Girl, Interrupted

Girl,
Interrupted

Susanna Kaysen

Turtle Bay Books
A Division of Random House
New York

All rights reserved under International and Pan-American
Copyright Conventions. Published in the United States by
Turtle Bay Books, a division of Random House, Inc., New York,
and simultaneously in Canada by Random House
of Canada Limited, Toronto.

Portions of this book, in slightly different form, appeared in *Agni*,
The Boston Review, and *Ploughshares*.

Grateful acknowledgment is made to American Psychiatric Press for permission to
reprint the entry for Borderline Personality Disorder from the American Psychiatric
Association's *Diagnostic and Statistical Manual of Mental Disorders, Third Edition, Revised*,
Washington, D.C., American Psychiatric Association, 1987.
Reprinted by permission.

The author is grateful to the Artists Foundation of Massachusetts and the
Corporation of Yaddo for their generosity.

Though this book is nonfiction, some of the names and distinguishing traits of
patients, doctors, and staff have been changed.

ISBN 0-679-42366-4

Manufactured in the United States of America

For Ingrid and Sanford

Girl, Interrupted

CASE RECORD FOLDER

. INSTITUTION	2. LAST NAME	FIRST NAME	MIDDLE INITIAL	3. REGISTER NUMBER
McLean Hospital	KAYSEN	Susanna	N.	

. LEGAL STATUS AT ADMISSION	5. LOCATION FROM WHICH ADMITTED	6. DATE ADMITTED
Voluntary	64 Wendell Street, Cambridge, Mass.	April 27, 1967

A. ESTABLISHED LEGAL STATUS	B. DATE	8. RECENT ADDRESS	9. SEX	10. COLOR
		same	F.	W.

1. ALIEN REG. NO.	12. TIME AT USUAL ADDRESS	13. USUAL ADDRESS	14. RELIGION	15. MARITAL ST
	Since 9/66	▓▓▓▓ Lane, Princeton, N. J.	Jewish	Single

6A. PORT OF ENTRY, IF FOREIGN BORN	B. DATE	17A. CITY OR TOWN OF BIRTH	B. STATE OR COUNTRY OF BIRTH	18. BIRTH DATE
		Boston	Mass.	18 yrs. Nov. 11, 1948

9A. IF NATURALIZED, PLACE	B. DATE	20A. FATHER'S NAME	B. FATHER'S BIRTH PLACE	21. U.S. MILITARY SERVICE
		Carl Kaysen	Philadelphia, Pa.	

2. EDUCATION	23A. MOTHER'S MAIDEN NAME	B. MOTHER'S BIRTH PLACE	24. SOCIAL SECURITY NO.
High School Graduate	Annette Neutra	Philadelphia, Pa.	Unknown

5. USUAL OCCUPATION OF PATIENT	26A. PERSON TO NOTIFY IN EMERGENCY	B. RELATIONSHIP
None	Mr. & Mrs. Carl Kaysen	Parents

7. USUAL OCCUPATION OF FATHER (PATIENT A MINOR)	C. ADDRESS ▓▓▓▓ Lane, Princeton, N. J.	D. TELEPHONE –AC609–
	Bus: Princeton Inst. for Adv. Studies (Director) AC609–	

8. USUAL OCCUPATION OF MOTHER (PATIENT A MINOR)	29A. PERSON TO NOTIFY IN EMERGENCY	B. RELATIONSHIP
	Dr. & Mrs. Sanford Gifford	Friends

0. DIAGNOSTIC IMPRESSION AT ADMISSION	C. ADDRESS ▓▓▓▓ Cambridge, Mass.	D. TELEPHONE Un–▓▓▓▓
Psychoneurotic depressive reaction. Personality pattern disturbance, mixed type. R/O Undifferentiated Schizophrenia.	31A. PERSON TO NOTIFY IN EMERGENCY	B. RELATIONSHIP
	C. ADDRESS —	D. TELEPHONE

2A. ESTABLISHED DIAGNOSIS, MENTAL DISORDER	33. ESTABLISHED DIAGNOSES, OTHER CONDITIONS
Borderline Personality	

B. QUALIFYING PHRASE

4. HISTORY OF TIME ON BOOKS OF INSTITUTIONS CARING FOR MENTAL DISORDER

A. NAME OF INSTITUTION	B. LOCATION	C. MONTH	D. YEAR	TO	E. MONTH	F. YEAR
None						

5. HISTORY OF OTHER HOSPITALIZATION

A. NAME OF HOSPITAL	B. LOCATION	C. YEAR	D. REASON
Mt. Auburn Hospital	Cambridge, Mass.	1965	(Stomach pumped)

Toward a Topography of the Parallel Universe

People ask, How did you get in there? What they really want to know is if they are likely to end up in there as well. I can't answer the real question. All I can tell them is, It's easy.

And it is easy to slip into a parallel universe. There are so many of them: worlds of the insane, the criminal, the crippled, the dying, perhaps of the dead as well. These worlds exist alongside this world and resemble it, but are not in it.

My roommate Georgina came in swiftly and totally, during her junior year at Vassar. She was in a theater watching a movie when a tidal wave of blackness broke over her head. The entire world was obliterated—for a few minutes. She knew she had gone crazy. She looked around the theater to see if it had happened to everyone, but all the other people were engrossed in the movie. She rushed out, because the darkness in the theater was too much when combined with the darkness in her head.

And after that? I asked her.

A lot of darkness, she said.

But most people pass over incrementally, making a series of perforations in the membrane between here and there until an opening exists. And who can resist an opening?

In the parallel universe the laws of physics are suspended. What goes up does not necessarily come down; a body at rest does not tend to stay at rest; and not every action can be counted on to provoke an equal and opposite reaction. Time, too, is different. It may run in circles, flow backward, skip about from now to then. The very arrangement of molecules is fluid: Tables can be clocks; faces, flowers.

These are facts you find out later, though.

Another odd feature of the parallel universe is that although it is invisible from this side, once you are in it you can easily see the world you came from. Sometimes the world you came from looks huge and menacing, quivering like a vast pile of jelly; at other times it is miniaturized and alluring, a-spin and shining in its orbit. Either way, it can't be discounted.

Every window on Alcatraz has a view of San Francisco.

The Taxi

"You have a pimple," said the doctor.

I'd hoped nobody would notice.

"You've been picking it," he went on.

When I'd woken that morning—early, so as to get to this appointment—the pimple had reached the stage of hard expectancy in which it begs to be picked. It was yearning for release. Freeing it from its little white dome, pressing until the blood ran, I felt a sense of accomplishment: I'd done all that could be done for this pimple.

"You've been picking at yourself," the doctor said.

I nodded. He was going to keep talking about it until I agreed with him, so I nodded.

"Have a boyfriend?" he asked.

I nodded to this too.

"Trouble with the boyfriend?" It wasn't a question, actually; he was already nodding for me. "Picking at yourself," he repeated. He popped out from behind his desk and lunged toward me. He was a taut fat man, tight-bellied and dark.

"You need a rest," he announced.

I did need a rest, particularly since I'd gotten up so early that morning in order to see this doctor, who lived out in the suburbs. I'd changed trains twice. And I would have to retrace my steps to get to my job. Just thinking of it made me tired.

"Don't you think?" He was still standing in front of me. "Don't you think you need a rest?"

"Yes," I said.

He strode off to the adjacent room, where I could hear him talking on the phone.

I have thought often of the next ten minutes—my last ten minutes. I had the impulse, once, to get up and leave through the door I'd entered, to walk the several blocks to the trolley stop and wait for the train that would take me back to my troublesome boyfriend, my job at the kitchen store. But I was too tired.

He strutted back into the room, busy, pleased with himself.

"I've got a bed for you," he said. "It'll be a rest. Just for a couple of weeks, okay?" He sounded conciliatory, or pleading, and I was afraid.

"I'll go Friday," I said. It was Tuesday; maybe by Friday I wouldn't want to go.

He bore down on me with his belly. "No. You go now."

I thought this was unreasonable. "I have a lunch date," I said.

"Forget it," he said. "You aren't going to lunch. You're going to the hospital." He looked triumphant.

It was very quiet out in the suburbs before eight in the morning. And neither of us had anything more to say. I heard the taxi pulling up in the doctor's driveway.

He took me by the elbow—pinched me between his large stout fingers—and steered me outside. Keeping hold of my arm, he opened the back door of the taxi and pushed me in. His big head was in the backseat with me for a moment. Then he slammed the door shut.

The driver rolled his window down halfway.

"Where to?"

Coatless in the chilly morning, planted on his sturdy legs in his driveway, the doctor lifted one arm to point at me.

"Take her to McLean," he said, "and don't let her out till you get there."

I let my head fall back against the seat and shut my eyes. I was glad to be riding in a taxi instead of having to wait for the train.

McLean Hospital: INQUIRY CONCERNING ADMISSION

Date: 4/27/67

Info obtained by: MA

PATIENT:

Name: Susanna Kaysen

Address: 64 Wendell St Camb

Tel:

Age: 18   Marital status: ___   Number of children: ___

REFERRING PERSON:

Name: Dr. ███████

Address:

Tel: ███████

Relationship (if physician, give specialty and will he follow? psych my ____

(NOTE: If relative called, give here name & address of physician to contact; or if physician called, give here name & address of relative or friend to contact:)

Name: Mr. Carl Kaysen   Institute for

Address ██████ Lane 609 921-   Advanced Stud

Princeton 921-   to 609 921-

Tel: ___   Relationship: ___   Dr. & Mrs. Sanborn █

                                        Hillside Pl. Camb.

                                        UN 4-████

DISCUSSION OF FINANCES (including rate):

enough for a yr   no. ins.

50,000 income

assets 60-70,000

IF PT IS TO BE ADMITTED: Expected arrival time: ___ ; mode of arrival: ___

will be accompanied by: alone   ward: SB II   leg. status: vol

case assigned to: ███████

REASON FOR REFERRAL: Needed McLean for 3 yrs

Profoundly depressed - suicidal

increasing patternless of life, promiscous

might kill self or get pregnant - former

these 3 yrs ██████ - she doesn't want to

                                        return

Daughter

Ran away from him 4 mos ago. Living in

boarding house in Camb -

Desparate -

PREVIOUS PSYCHIATRIC TREATMENT: Where: ___

Type: Eval ( ) Therapy ( ) Other (what) ___ when: ___ by whom: ___

PHYSICAL HANDICAPS: ___ **ALLERGIES:** ___ **SUICIDAL** (✓) ASSAULTIVE ( ) ESCAPE ( )

IF FOLLOW-UP NEEDED: (give summary here; details on separate sheet; sign your name)

IF PATIENT NOT ADMITTED: (give summary of reasons; sign your name)

Revised - 1/28/64   F-46

INTER OFFICE MEMORANDUM

TO   Record Room   Date June 15, 1967
          Dr. ████████████

FROM   Dr. ██████████████████

SUBJECT   Susanna Kaysen

Susanna Kaysen was seen by me on April 27, 1967; following my evaluation which
extended over three hours, I referred her to McLean Hospital for admission.

My decision was based on:

  1. The chaotic unplanned life of the patient at present with progressive
      decompensation and reversal of sleep cycle.

  2. Severe depression and hopelessness and suicidal ideas.

  3. History of suicidal attempts.

  4. No therapy and no plan at present. Immersion in fantasy, progressive
      withdrawal and isolation.

The patient had been seen in psychotherapy by Dr. ████████████████. At no time
did I have her ih therapy, and the patient knew that I was not a potential
therapist.

lsk

Etiology

This person is (pick one):

1. on a perilous journey from which we can learn much when he or she returns;
2. possessed by (pick one):
   a) the gods,
   b) God (that is, a prophet),
   c) some bad spirits, demons, or devils,
   d) the Devil;
3. a witch;
4. bewitched (variant of 2);
5. bad, and must be isolated and punished;
6. ill, and must be isolated and treated by (pick one):
   a) purging and leeches,
   b) removing the uterus if the person has one,
   c) electric shock to the brain,
   d) cold sheets wrapped tight around the body,
   e) Thorazine or Stelazine;
7. ill, and must spend the next seven years talking about it;
8. a victim of society's low tolerance for deviant behavior;
9. sane in an insane world;
10. on a perilous journey from which he or she may never return.

Fire

One girl among us had set herself on fire. She used gasoline. She was too young to drive at the time. I wondered how she'd gotten hold of it. Had she walked to her neighborhood garage and told them her father's car had run out of gas? I couldn't look at her without thinking about it.

I think the gasoline had settled in her collarbones, forming pools there beside her shoulders, because her neck and cheeks were scarred the most. The scars were thick ridges, alternating bright pink and white, in stripes up from her neck. They were so tough and wide that she couldn't turn her head, but had to swivel her entire upper torso if she wanted to see a person standing next to her.

Scar tissue has no character. It's not like skin. It doesn't show age or illness or pallor or tan. It has no pores, no hair, no wrinkles. It's like a slipcover. It shields and disguises what's beneath. That's why we grow it; we have something to hide.

Her name was Polly. This name must have seemed ridiculous to her in the days—or months—when she was planning to set herself on fire, but it suited her well in her slipcovered, survivor life. She was never unhappy. She was kind and comforting to those who were unhappy. She never

16

complained. She always had time to listen to other people's complaints. She was faultless, in her impermeable tight pink-and-white casing. Whatever had driven her, whispered "Die!" in her once-perfect, now-scarred ear, she had immolated it.

Why did she do it? Nobody knew. Nobody dared to ask. Because—what courage! Who had the courage to burn herself? Twenty aspirin, a little slit alongside the veins of the arm, maybe even a bad half hour standing on a roof: We've all had those. And somewhat more dangerous things, like putting a gun in your mouth. But you put it there, you taste it, it's cold and greasy, your finger is on the trigger, and you find that a whole world lies between this moment and the moment you've been planning, when you'll pull the trigger. That world defeats you. You put the gun back in the drawer. You'll have to find another way.

What was that moment like for her? The moment she lit the match. Had she already tried roofs and guns and aspirin? Or was it just an inspiration?

I had an inspiration once. I woke up one morning and I knew that today I had to swallow fifty aspirin. It was my task: my job for the day. I lined them up on my desk and took them one by one, counting. But it's not the same as what she did. I could have stopped, at ten, or at thirty. And I could have done what I did do, which was go onto the street and faint. Fifty aspirin is a lot of aspirin, but going onto the street and fainting is like putting the gun back in the drawer.

She lit the match.

Where? In the garage at home, where she wouldn't set

anything else on fire? Out in a field? In the high school gym? In an empty swimming pool?

Somebody found her, but not for a while.

Who would kiss a person like that, a person with no skin?

She was eighteen before this thought occurred to her. She'd spent a year with us. Other people stormed and screamed and cringed and cried; Polly watched and smiled. She sat by people who were frightened, and her presence calmed them. Her smile wasn't mean, it was understanding. Life was hellish, she knew that. But, her smile hinted, she'd burned all that out of her. Her smile was a little bit superior: We wouldn't have the courage to burn it out of ourselves— but she understood that too. Everyone was different. People just did what they could.

One morning somebody was crying, but mornings were often noisy: fights about getting up on time and complaints about nightmares. Polly was so quiet, so unobtrusive a presence, that we didn't notice she wasn't at breakfast. After breakfast, we could still hear crying.

"Who's crying?"

Nobody knew.

And at lunch, there was still crying.

"It's Polly," said Lisa, who knew everything.

"Why?"

But even Lisa didn't know why.

At dusk the crying changed to screaming. Dusk is a dangerous time. At first she screamed, "Aaaaaah!" and "Eeeeeh!" Then she started to scream words.

"My face! My face! *My face!*"

We could hear other voices shushing her, murmuring comfort, but she continued to scream her two words long into the night.

Lisa said, "Well, I've been expecting this for a while."

And then I think we all realized what fools we'd been.

We might get out sometime, but she was locked up forever in that body.

Freedom

Lisa had run away again. We were sad, because she kept our spirits up. She was funny. Lisa! I can't think of her without smiling, even now.

The worst was that she was always caught and dragged back, dirty, with wild eyes that had seen freedom. She would curse her captors, and even the tough old-timers had to laugh at the names she made up.

"Cheese-pussy!" And another favorite, "You schizophrenic bat!"

Usually, they found her within a day. She couldn't get far on foot, with no money. But this time she seemed to have lucked out. On the third day I heard someone in the nursing station saying "APB" into the phone: all points bulletin.

Lisa wouldn't be hard to identify. She rarely ate and she never slept, so she was thin and yellow, the way people get when they don't eat, and she had huge bags under her eyes. She had long dark dull hair that she fastened with a silver clip. She had the longest fingers I've ever seen.

This time, when they brought her back, they were almost as angry as she was. Two big men had her arms, and a third guy had her by the hair, pulling so that Lisa's eyes bugged out. Everybody was quiet, including Lisa. They took her down to the end of the hall, to seclusion, while we watched.

We watched a lot of things.

We watched Cynthia come back crying from electroshock once a week. We watched Polly shiver after being wrapped in ice-cold sheets. One of the worst things we watched, though, was Lisa coming out of seclusion two days later.

To begin with, they'd cut her nails down to the quick. She'd had beautiful nails, which she worked on, polishing, shaping, buffing. They said her nails were "sharps."

And they'd taken away her belt. Lisa always wore a cheap beaded belt—the kind made by Indians on reservations. It was green, with red triangles on it, and it had belonged to her brother Jonas, the only one in her family still in touch with her. Her mother and father wouldn't visit her because she was a sociopath, or so said Lisa. They took away the belt so she couldn't hang herself.

They didn't understand that Lisa would never hang herself.

They let her out of seclusion, they gave her back her belt, and her nails started to grow in again, but Lisa didn't come back. She just sat and watched TV with the worst of us.

Lisa had never watched TV. She'd had nothing but scorn for those who did. "It's shit!" she'd yell, sticking her head into the TV room. "You're already like robots. It's making you worse." Sometimes she turned off the TV and stood in front of it, daring somebody to turn it on. But the TV audience was mostly catatonics and depressives, who were disinclined to move. After five minutes, which was about as long as she could stand still, Lisa would be off on another project, and when the person on checks came around, she would turn the TV on again.

Since Lisa hadn't slept for the two years she'd been with us, the nurses had given up telling her to go to bed. Instead, she had a chair of her own in the hallway, just like the night staff, where she'd sit and work on her nails. She made wonderful cocoa, and at three o'clock in the morning she made cocoa for the night staff and anybody else who was up. She was calmer at night.

Once I asked her, "Lisa, how come you don't rush around and yell at night?"

"I need rest too," she said. "Just because I don't sleep doesn't mean I don't rest."

Lisa always knew what she needed. She'd say, "I need a vacation from this place," and then she'd run away. When she got back, we'd ask her how it was out there.

"It's a mean world," she'd say. She was usually glad enough to be back. "There's nobody to take care of you out there."

Now she said nothing. She spent all her time in the TV room. She watched prayers and test patterns and hours of late-night talk shows and early-morning news. Her chair in the hall was unoccupied, and nobody got cocoa.

"Are you giving Lisa something?" I asked the person on checks.

"You know we can't discuss medication with patients."

I asked the head nurse. I'd known her awhile, since before she was the head nurse.

But she acted as though she'd always been the head nurse. "We can't discuss medication—you know that."

"Why bother asking," said Georgina. "She's completely blotto. Of course they're giving her something."

Cynthia didn't think so. "She still walks okay," she said.

"I don't," said Polly. She didn't. She walked with her arms stuck out in front of her, her red-and-white hands drooping from her wrists and her feet shuffling along the floor. The cold packs hadn't worked, she still screamed all night until they put her on something.

"It took a while," I said. "You walked okay when they started it."

"Now I don't," said Polly. She looked at her hands.

I asked Lisa if they were giving her something, but she wouldn't look at me.

And this way we all passed through a month or two, Lisa and the catatonics in the TV room, Polly walking like a motorized corpse, Cynthia crying after electroshock ("I'm not sad," she explained to me, "but I can't help crying"), and me and Georgina in our double suite. We were considered the healthiest.

When spring came Lisa began spending a little more time outside the TV room. She spent it in the bathroom, to be exact, but at least it was a change.

I asked the person on checks, "What's she doing in the bathroom?"

This was a new person. "Am I supposed to open bathroom doors too?"

I did what we often did to new people. "Somebody could hang herself in there in a minute! Where do you think you are, anyhow? A boarding school?" Then I put my face close to hers. They didn't like that, touching us.

I noticed Lisa went to a different bathroom every time. There were four, and she made the circuit daily. She didn't look good. Her belt was hanging off her and she looked yellower than usual.

"Maybe she's got dysentery," I said to Georgina. But Georgina thought she was just blotto.

One morning in May we were eating breakfast when we heard a door slam. Then Lisa appeared in the kitchen.

"Later for that TV," she said. She poured herself a big cup of coffee, just as she used to do in the mornings, and sat down at the table. She smiled at us, and we smiled back. "Wait," she said.

We heard feet running and voices saying things like "What in the world . . ." and "How in the world . . ." Then the head nurse came into the kitchen.

"You did this," she said to Lisa.

We went to see what it was.

She had wrapped all the furniture, some of it holding catatonics, and the TV and the sprinkler system on the ceiling in toilet paper. Yards and yards of it floated and dangled, bunched and draped on everything, everywhere. It was magnificent.

"She wasn't blotto," I said to Georgina. "She was plotting."

We had a good summer, and Lisa told us lots of stories about what she'd done those three days she was free.

The Secret of Life

One day I had a visitor. I was in the TV room watching Lisa watch TV, when a nurse came in to tell me.

"You've got a visitor," she said. "A man."

It wasn't my troublesome boyfriend. First of all, he wasn't my boyfriend anymore. How could a person who was locked up have a boyfriend? Anyhow, he couldn't bear coming here. His mother had been in a loony bin too, it turned out, and he couldn't bear being reminded of it.

It wasn't my father; he was busy.

It wasn't my high school English teacher; he'd been fired and moved to North Carolina.

I went to see who it was.

He was standing at a window in the living room, looking out: giraffe-tall, with slumpy academic shoulders, wrists sticking out of his jacket, and pale hair that shot out from his head in a corona. He turned around when he heard me come in.

It was Jim Watson. I was happy to see him, because, in the fifties, he had discovered the secret of life, and now, perhaps, he would tell it to me.

"Jim!" I said.

He drifted toward me. He drifted and wobbled and faded

out while he was supposed to be talking to people, and I'd always liked him for that.

"You look fine," he told me.

"What did you expect?" I asked.

He shook his head.

"What do they do to you in here?" He was whispering.

"Nothing," I said. "They don't do anything."

"It's terrible here," he said.

The living room was a particularly terrible part of our ward. It was huge and jammed with huge vinyl-covered armchairs that farted when anyone sat down.

"It's not really that bad," I said, but I was used to it and he wasn't.

He drifted toward the window again and looked out. After a while he beckoned me over with one of his long arms.

"Look." He pointed at something.

"At what?"

"That." He was pointing at a car. It was a red sports car, maybe an MG. "That's mine," he said. He'd won the Nobel Prize, so probably he'd bought this car with the money.

"Nice," I said. "Very nice."

Now he was whispering again. "We could leave," he whispered.

"Hunh?"

"You and me, we could leave."

"In the car, you mean?" I felt confused. Was this the secret of life? Running away was the secret of life?

"They'd come after me," I said.

"It's fast," he said. "I could get you out of here."

Suddenly I felt protective of him. "Thanks," I said. "Thanks for offering. It's sweet of you."

"Don't you want to go?" He leaned toward me. "We could go to England."

"England?" What did England have to do with anything? "I can't go to England," I said.

"You could be a governess," he said.

For ten seconds I imagined this other life, which began when I stepped into Jim Watson's red car and we sped out of the hospital and on to the airport. The governess part was hazy. The whole thing, in fact, was hazy. The vinyl chairs, the security screens, the buzzing of the nursing-station door: Those things were clear.

"I'm here now, Jim," I said. "I think I've got to stay here."

"Okay." He didn't seem miffed. He looked around the room one last time and shook his head.

I stayed at the window. After a few minutes I saw him get into his red car and drive off, leaving little puffs of sporty exhaust behind him. Then I went back to the TV room.

"Hi, Lisa," I said. I was glad to see she was still there.

"Rnnn," said Lisa.

Then we settled in for some more TV.

Politics

In our parallel world, things happened that had not yet happened in the world we'd come from. When they finally happened outside, we found them familiar because versions of them had been performed in front of us. It was as if we were a provincial audience, New Haven to the real world's New York, where history could try out its next spectacle.

For instance, the story of Georgina's boyfriend, Brad, and the sugar.

They'd met in the cafeteria. Brad was dark and good-looking in a flat, all-American way. What made him irresistible was his rage. He was enraged about almost everything and glowed with anger. Georgina explained that his father was the problem.

"His father's a spy, and Brad's mad that he can never be as tough as his father."

I was more interested in Brad's father than in Brad's problem.

"A spy for us?" I asked.

"Of course," said Georgina, but she wouldn't say more.

Brad and Georgina would sit on the floor of our room and whisper. I was supposed to leave them alone, and usually I did. One day, though, I decided to stick around and find out about Brad's father.

Brad loved talking about him. "He lives in Miami, so he can get over to Cuba. He invaded Cuba. He's killed dozens of people, with his bare hands. He knows who killed the president."

"Did he kill the president?" I asked.

"I don't think so," said Brad.

Brad's last name was Barker.

I have to admit I didn't believe a word of what Brad said. After all, he was a crazy seventeen-year-old who got so violent that it took two big aides to hold him down. Sometimes he'd be locked on his ward for a week and Georgina couldn't get in to see him. Then he'd simmer down and resume his visits on the floor of our room.

Brad's father had two friends who particularly impressed Brad: Liddy and Hunt. "Those guys will do anything!" Brad said. He said this often, and he seemed worried about it.

Georgina didn't like my pestering Brad about his father; she ignored me as I sat on the floor with them. But I couldn't resist.

"Like what?" I asked him. "What kinds of things will they do?"

"I can't reveal," said Brad.

Shortly after this he lapsed into a violent phase that went on for several weeks.

Georgina was at a loose end without Brad's visits. Because I felt partly responsible for his absence, I offered various distractions. "Let's redecorate the room," I said. "Let's play Scrabble." Or "Let's cook things."

Cooking things was what appealed to Georgina. "Let's make caramels," she said.

29

I was surprised that two people in a kitchen could make caramels. I thought of them as a mass-production item, like automobiles, for which complicated machinery was needed.

But, according to Georgina, all we needed was a frying pan and sugar.

"When it's caramelized," she said, "we pour it into little balls on waxed paper."

The nurses thought it was cute that we were cooking. "Practicing for when you and Brad get married?" one asked.

"I don't think Brad is the marrying kind," said Georgina.

Even someone who's never made caramels knows how hot sugar has to be before it caramelizes. That's how hot it was when the pan slipped and I poured half the sugar onto Georgina's hand, which was holding the waxed paper straight.

I screamed and screamed, but Georgina didn't make a sound. The nurses ran in and produced ice and unguents and wrappings, and I kept screaming, and Georgina did nothing. She stood still with her candied hand stretched out in front of her.

I can't remember if it was E. Howard Hunt or G. Gordon Liddy who said, during the Watergate hearings, that he'd nightly held his hand in a candle flame till his palm burned to assure himself he could stand up to torture.

Whoever it was, we knew about it already: the Bay of Pigs, the seared skin, the bare-handed killers who'd do anything. We'd seen the previews, Brad, Georgina, and I, along with an audience of nurses whose reviews ran something like this: "Patient lacked affect after accident"; "Patient continues fantasy that father is CIA operative with dangerous friends."

If You Lived Here,
You'd Be Home Now

Daisy was a seasonal event. She came before Thanksgiving and stayed through Christmas every year. Some years she came for her birthday in May as well.

She always got a single. "Would anybody like to share?" the head nurse asked at our weekly Hall Meeting one November morning. It was a tense moment. Georgina and I, who already shared, were free to enjoy the confusion.

"Me! Me!" Somebody who was a Martian's girlfriend and also had a little penis of her own, which she was eager to show off, raised a hand; nobody wanted to share with her.

"I would if somebody would want to but of course nobody would want to so I wouldn't want to force somebody to want to." This was Cynthia, who'd started talking like that after six months of shock.

Polly to the rescue: "I'll share with you, Cynthia."

But that didn't solve the problem, because Polly was in a double herself. Her roommate was a new anorexic named Janet who was scheduled for force feedings the moment she dropped below seventy-five.

Lisa leaned toward me. "I watched her on the scale yesterday: seventy-eight," she said loudly. "She'll be on the tube by the weekend."

"Seventy-eight is the perfect weight," said Janet. She'd said the same about eighty-three and seventy-nine, though, so nobody wanted to share with her, either.

In the end a couple of catatonics were teamed up and Daisy's room was ready for her arrival on November fifteenth.

Daisy had two passions: laxatives and chicken. Every morning she presented herself at the nursing station and drummed her fingers, pale and stained with nicotine, on the counter, impatient for laxatives.

"I want my Colace," she would hiss. "I want my Ex-Lax."

If someone was standing near her, she would jab her elbow into that person's side or step on her foot. Daisy hated anyone to be near her.

Twice a week her squat potato-face father brought a whole chicken roasted by her mother and wrapped in aluminum foil. Daisy would hold the chicken in her lap and fondle it through the foil, darting her eyes around the room, eager for her father to leave so she could get going on the chicken. But Daisy's father wanted to stay as long as possible, because he was in love with Daisy.

Lisa explained it. "He can't believe he produced her. He wants to fuck her to make sure she's real."

"But she smells," Polly objected. She smelled, of course, like chicken and shit.

"She didn't always smell," said Lisa.

I thought Lisa was right, because I'd noticed that Daisy was sexy. Even though she smelled and glowered and hissed and poked, she had a spark the rest of us lacked. She wore shorts and tank tops to display her pale wiry limbs, and when she ambled down the hall in the morning to get her laxatives, she swung her ass in insouciant half-circles.

The Martian's girlfriend was in love with her too. She followed her down the hall crooning, "Want to see my penis?" To which Daisy would hiss, "I shit on your penis."

Nobody had ever been in Daisy's room. Lisa was determined to get in. She had a plan.

"Man, am I constipated," she said for three days. "Wow." On the fourth day she got some Ex-Lax out of the head nurse. "Didn't work," she reported the next morning. "Got anything stronger?"

"How about castor oil?" said the head nurse. She was overworked.

"This place is a fascist snake pit," said Lisa. "Give me a double dose of Ex-Lax."

Now she had six Ex-Lax and she was ready to bargain. She stood in front of Daisy's door.

"Hey, Daisy," she called. "Hey, Daisy." She kicked the door.

"Fuck off," said Daisy.

"Hey, Daisy."

Daisy hissed.

Lisa leaned close to the door. "I got something you want," she said.

"Bullshit," said Daisy. Then she opened the door.

Georgina and I had been watching from down the hall. When Daisy opened the door we craned our necks, but it was too dark in Daisy's room to see anything. When the door shut behind Lisa, a strange sweet smell wafted briefly into the hall.

Lisa didn't come out for a long time. We gave up waiting and went over to the cafeteria for lunch.

Lisa gave her report during the evening news. She stood in front of the TV and spoke loud enough to drown out Walter Cronkite.

"Daisy's room is full of chicken," she said. "She eats chicken in there. She has a special method she showed me. She peels all the meat off because she likes to keep the carcasses whole. Even the wings—she peels the meat off them. Then she puts the carcass on the floor next to the last carcass. She has about nine now. She says when she's got fourteen it's time to leave."

"Did she give you any chicken?" I asked.

"I didn't want any of her disgusting chicken."

"Why does she do it?" Georgina asked.

"Hey, man," said Lisa, "I don't know everything."

"What about the laxatives?" Polly wanted to know.

"Needs 'em. Needs 'em because of all the chicken."

"There's more to this than meets the eye," said Georgina.

"Listen! I got access," said Lisa. The discussion degenerated quickly after that.

Within the week there was more news about Daisy. Her father had bought her an apartment for Christmas. "A love nest," Lisa called it.

Daisy was pleased with herself and spent more time out of her room, hoping that someone would ask her about the apartment. Georgina obliged.

"How big is the apartment, Daisy?"

"One bedroom, L-shaped living room, eat-in chicken."

"You mean eat-in kitchen?"

"That's what I said, asshole."

"Where's the apartment, Daisy?"

"Near the Mass. General."

"On the way to the airport, like?"

"Near the Mass. General." Daisy didn't want to admit it was on the way to the airport.

"What do you like best about it?"

Daisy shut her eyes and paused, relishing her favorite part. "The sign."

"What does the sign say?"

" 'If you lived here, you'd be home now.' " She clenched her hands with excitement. "See, every day people will drive past and read that sign and think, 'Yeah, if I lived here I'd be home now,' and I *will* be home. Motherfuckers."

Daisy left early that year, to spend Christmas in her apartment.

"She'll be back," said Lisa. But Lisa for once was wrong.

One afternoon in May we were called to a special Hall Meeting.

"Girls," said the head nurse, "I have some sad news." We all leaned forward. "Daisy committed suicide yesterday."

"Was she in her apartment?" asked Georgina.

"Did she shoot herself?" asked Polly.

"Who's Daisy? Do I know Daisy?" asked the Martian's girlfriend.

"Did she leave a note?" I asked.

"The details aren't important," said the head nurse.

"It was her birthday, wasn't it?" asked Lisa. The head nurse nodded.

We all observed a moment of silence for Daisy.

My Suicide

Suicide is a form of murder—premeditated murder. It isn't something you do the first time you think of doing it. It takes getting used to. And you need the means, the opportunity, the motive. A successful suicide demands good organization and a cool head, both of which are usually incompatible with the suicidal state of mind.

It's important to cultivate detachment. One way to do this is to practice imagining yourself dead, or in the process of dying. If there's a window, you must imagine your body falling out the window. If there's a knife, you must imagine the knife piercing your skin. If there's a train coming, you must imagine your torso flattened under its wheels. These exercises are necessary to achieving the proper distance.

The motive is paramount. Without a strong motive, you're sunk.

My motives were weak: an American-history paper I didn't want to write and the question I'd asked months earlier, Why not kill myself? Dead, I wouldn't have to write the paper. Nor would I have to keep debating the question.

The debate was wearing me out. Once you've posed that question, it won't go away. I think many people kill themselves simply to stop the debate about whether they will or they won't.

Anything I thought or did was immediately drawn into the debate. Made a stupid remark—why not kill myself? Missed the bus—better put an end to it all. Even the good got in there. I liked that movie—maybe I shouldn't kill myself.

Actually, it was only part of myself I wanted to kill: the part that wanted to kill herself, that dragged me into the suicide debate and made every window, kitchen implement, and subway station a rehearsal for tragedy.

I didn't figure this out, though, until after I'd swallowed the fifty aspirin.

I had a boyfriend named Johnny who wrote me love poems—good ones. I called him up, said I was going to kill myself, left the phone off the hook, took my fifty aspirin, and realized it was a mistake. Then I went out to get some milk, which my mother had asked me to do before I took the aspirin.

Johnny called the police. They went to my house and told my mother what I'd done. She turned up in the A&P on Mass. Ave. just as I was about to pass out over the meat counter.

As I walked the five blocks to the A&P I was gripped by humiliation and regret. I'd made a mistake and I was going to die because of it. Perhaps I even deserved to die because of it. I began to cry about my death. For a moment, I felt compassion for myself and all the unhappiness I contained. Then things started to blur and whiz. By the time I reached the store, the world had been reduced to a narrow, throbbing tunnel. I'd lost my peripheral vision, my ears were ringing, my pulse was pounding. The bloody chops and steaks straining against their plastic wrappings were the last things I saw clearly.

Having my stomach pumped brought me around. They took a long tube and put it slowly up my nose and down the back of my throat. That was like being choked to death. Then they began to pump. That was like having blood drawn on a massive scale—the suction, the sense of tissue collapsing and touching itself in a way it shouldn't, the nausea as all that was inside was pulled out. It was a good deterrent. Next time, I decided, I certainly wouldn't take aspirin.

But when they were done, I wondered if there would be a next time. I felt good. I wasn't dead, yet something was dead. Perhaps I'd managed my peculiar objective of partial suicide. I was lighter, airier than I'd been in years.

My airiness lasted for months. I did some of my homework. I stopped seeing Johnny and took up with my English teacher, who wrote even better poems, though not to me. I went to New York with him; he took me to the Frick to see the Vermeers.

The only odd thing was that suddenly I was a vegetarian.

I associated meat with suicide, because of passing out at the meat counter. But I knew there was more to it.

The meat was bruised, bleeding, and imprisoned in a tight wrapping. And, though I had a six-month respite from thinking about it, so was I.

Elementary Topography

Perhaps it's still unclear how I ended up in there. It must have been something more than a pimple. I didn't mention that I'd never seen that doctor before, that he decided to put me away after only fifteen minutes. Twenty, maybe. What about me was so deranged that in less than half an hour a doctor would pack me off to the nuthouse? He tricked me, though: a couple of weeks. It was closer to two years. I was eighteen.

I signed myself in. I had to, because I was of age. It was that or a court order, though they could never have gotten a court order against me. I didn't know that, so I signed myself in.

I wasn't a danger to society. Was I a danger to myself? The fifty aspirin—but I've explained them. They were metaphorical. I wanted to get rid of a certain aspect of my character. I was performing a kind of self-abortion with those aspirin. It worked for a while. Then it stopped; but I had no heart to try again.

Take it from his point of view. It was 1967. Even in lives like his, professional lives lived out in the suburbs behind shrubbery, there was a strange undertow, a tug from the other world—the drifting, drugged-out, no-last-name youth universe—that knocked people off balance. One could call it "threatening," to use his language. What are these kids *doing?* And then one of them walks into his office wearing a skirt the size of a napkin, with a mottled chin and speaking in monosyllables. Doped up, he figures. He looks again at the name jotted on the notepad in front of him. Didn't he meet her parents at a party two years ago? Harvard faculty—or was it MIT? Her boots are worn down but her coat's a good one. It's a mean world out there, as Lisa would say. He can't in good conscience send her back into it, to become flotsam on the subsocietal tide that washes up now and then in his office, depositing others like her. A form of preventive medicine.

Am I being too kind to him? A few years ago I read he'd been accused of sexual harassment by a former patient. But that's been happening a lot these days; it's become fashionable to accuse doctors. Maybe it was just too early in the morning for him as well as for me, and he couldn't think of what else to do. Maybe, most likely, he was just covering his ass.

My point of view is harder to explain. I went. First I went to his office, then I got into the taxi, then I walked up the stone steps to the Administration Building of McLean Hospital, and, if I remember correctly, sat in a chair for fifteen minutes waiting to sign my freedom away.

Several preconditions are necessary if you are going to do such a thing.

I was having a problem with patterns. Oriental rugs, tile floors, printed curtains, things like that. Supermarkets were especially bad, because of the long, hypnotic checkerboard aisles. When I looked at these things, I saw other things within them. That sounds as though I was hallucinating, and I wasn't. I knew I was looking at a floor or a curtain. But all patterns seemed to contain potential representations, which in a dizzying array would flicker briefly to life. That could be . . . a forest, a flock of birds, my second-grade class picture. Well, it wasn't—it was a rug, or whatever it was, but my glimpses of the other things it might be were exhausting. Reality was getting too dense.

Something also was happening to my perceptions of people. When I looked at someone's face, I often did not maintain an unbroken connection to the concept of a face. Once you start parsing a face, it's a peculiar item: squishy, pointy, with lots of air vents and wet spots. This was the reverse of my problem with patterns. Instead of seeing too much meaning, I didn't see any meaning.

But I wasn't simply going nuts, tumbling down a shaft into Wonderland. It was my misfortune—or salvation—to be at all times perfectly conscious of my misperceptions of reality. I never "believed" anything I saw or thought I saw. Not only that, I correctly understood each new weird activity.

Now, I would say to myself, you are feeling alienated from people and unlike other people, therefore you are projecting your discomfort onto them. When you look at a face, you see a blob of rubber because you are worried that your face is a blob of rubber.

This clarity made me able to behave normally, which posed some interesting questions. Was everybody seeing this stuff and acting as though they weren't? Was insanity just a matter of dropping the act? If some people didn't see these things, what was the matter with them? Were they blind or something? These questions had me unsettled.

Something had been peeled back, a covering or shell that works to protect us. I couldn't decide whether the covering was something on me or something attached to every thing in the world. It didn't matter, really; wherever it had been, it wasn't there anymore.

And this was the main precondition, that anything might be something else. Once I'd accepted that, it followed that I might be mad, or that someone might think me mad. How could I say for certain that I wasn't, if I couldn't say for certain that a curtain wasn't a mountain range?

I have to admit, though, that I knew I wasn't mad.

It was a different precondition that tipped the balance: the state of contrariety. My ambition was to negate. The world, whether dense or hollow, provoked only my negations. When I was supposed to be awake, I was asleep; when I was supposed to speak, I was silent; when a pleasure offered itself to me, I avoided it. My hunger, my thirst, my loneliness and boredom and fear were all weapons aimed at my enemy, the world. They didn't matter a whit to the world, of course, and they tormented me, but I got a gruesome satisfaction from my sufferings. They proved my existence. All my integrity seemed to lie in saying No.

So the opportunity to be incarcerated was just too good to resist. It was a very big No—the biggest No this side of suicide.

Perverse reasoning. But back of that perversity, I knew I wasn't mad and that they wouldn't keep me there, locked up in a loony bin.

1967	
April 27	ABSTRACT FROM VOLUNTARY APPLICATION: Patient withdrew to her room, ate very little, did not work or study and contemplated jumping into the river. She signed this voluntary application fully realizing the nature of her act.

██████████████ M. D./h
Director

Applied Topography

Two locked doors with a five-foot space between them where you had to stand while the nurse relocked the first door and unlocked the second.

Just inside, three phone booths. Then a couple of single rooms and the living room and eat-in kitchen. This arrangement ensured a good first impression for visitors.

Once you turned the corner past the living room, though, things changed.

A long, long hallway: too long. Seven or eight double rooms on one side, the nursing station centered on the other, flanked by the conference room and hydrotherapy tub room. Lunatics to the left, staff to the right. The toilets and shower rooms were also to the right, as though the staff claimed oversight of our most private acts.

A blackboard with our twenty-odd names in green chalk and spaces after each where we, in white chalk, entered our destination, departure time, and time of return whenever we left the ward. The blackboard hung directly across from the nursing station. When someone was restricted to the ward, the head nurse wrote RESTRICTED in green chalk beside the name. We got advance warning of an admission when a new name appeared on the list—sometimes as much as a day before the person of that name appeared on the hall. The discharged and the dead stayed on the list for a while in silent memoriam.

At the end of the terrible hall, the terrible TV room. We liked it. At least, we preferred it to the living room. It was messy, noisy, smoky, and, most important, it was on the left, lunatic side of things. As far as we were concerned, the living room belonged to the staff. We often agitated to move our weekly Hall Meeting from the living room to the TV room; it never happened.

After the TV room, another turn in the hall. Two more singles, one double, a toilet, and seclusion.

The seclusion room was the size of the average suburban bathroom. Its only window was the chicken-wire-enforced one in the door that allowed people to look in and see what you were up to. You couldn't get up to much in there. The only thing in it was a bare mattress on the green linoleum floor. The walls were chipped, as though somebody had been at them with fingernails or teeth. The seclusion room was supposed to be soundproof. It wasn't.

You could pop into the seclusion room, shut the door, and yell for a while. When you were done you could open the door and leave. Yelling in the TV room or the hall was "acting out" and was not a good idea. But yelling in the seclusion room was fine.

You could also "request" to be locked into the seclusion room. Not many people made that request. You had to "request" to get out too. A nurse would look through the chicken wire and decide if you were ready to come out. Somewhat like looking at a cake through the glass of the oven door.

The seclusion-room etiquette was, If you weren't locked in, anybody could join you. A nurse could interrupt your yelling to try to find out why you were yelling, or some other crazy person could come in and start yelling too. Hence the "request" business. Freedom was the price of privacy.

The real purpose of the seclusion room, though, was to quarantine people who'd gone bananas. As a group we maintained a certain level of noisiness and misery. Anyone who sustained a higher level for more than a few hours was put in seclusion. Otherwise, the staff reasoned, we would all turn up the volume on our nuttiness, and the staff would lose control. There were no objective criteria for deciding to put someone into seclusion. It was relative, like the grading curve in high school.

Seclusion worked. After a day or a night in there with nothing to do, most people calmed down. If they didn't, they went to maximum security.

Our double-locked doors, our steel-mesh window screens, our kitchen stocked with plastic knives and locked unless a nurse was with us, our bathroom doors that didn't lock: All this was medium security. Maximum security was another world.

The Prelude to Ice Cream

The hospital was on a hill outside of town, the way hospitals are in movies about the insane. Our hospital was famous and had housed many great poets and singers. Did the hospital specialize in poets and singers, or was it that poets and singers specialized in madness?

Ray Charles was the most famous ex-patient. We all hoped he'd return and serenade us from the window of the drug-rehabilitation ward. He never did.

We had the Taylor family, though. James graduated to a different hospital before I arrived, but Kate and Livingston were there. In Ray Charles's absence, their North Carolina–twanged blues made us sad enough. When you're sad you need to hear your sorrow structured into sound.

Robert Lowell also didn't come while I was there. Sylvia Plath had come and gone.

What is it about meter and cadence and rhythm that makes their makers mad?

The grounds were large and beautifully planted. They were pristine as well, since we were almost never allowed to walk around. But now and then, for a special treat, we were taken through them on the way to get ice cream.

The group had an atomic structure: a nucleus of nuts

surrounded by darting, nervous nurse-electrons charged with our protection. Or with protecting the residents of Belmont from us.

The residents were well heeled. Most worked as engineers or technocrats along the Technology Highway, Route 128. The important other type of Belmont resident was the John Bircher. The John Birch Society lay as far to the east of Belmont as the hospital lay to the west. We saw the two institutions as variations on each other; doubtless the Birchers did not see it this way. But between us we had Belmont surrounded. The engineers knew this, and they took care not to stare when we came into the ice cream parlor.

Saying that we traveled with a group of nurses does not fully explain the situation. A complex system of "privileges" determined how many nurses accompanied each patient, and whether a patient could leave the grounds in the first place.

The privileges started at no privileges: restricted to the ward. This was often Lisa's condition. Sometimes she was bumped up to the next rung, two-to-ones. That meant she could leave the ward if she had two nurses with her, though only to go to the cafeteria or occupational therapy. Even with our high staff-to-patient ratio, two-to-ones often meant restricted to the ward. Two nurses could rarely be spared to take Lisa by the elbows and hustle her over to dinner. Then there were one-to-ones: a nurse and patient bound together like Siamese twins. Some patients were on one-to-ones even on the ward, which was like having a page or valet. Or like having a bad conscience. It depended on the nurse. A lousy nurse on one-to-ones could be a problem; it was usually a long-term assignment, so the nurse could get to understand her patient.

The gradations were Byzantine. One-to-twos (one nurse, two patients) led to group (three or four patients and one nurse). If you behaved in group, you got something called destination privileges: This meant telephoning the head nurse the moment you arrived at wherever you were going to let her know you were there. You had to call before coming back, too, so she could calculate time and distance in case you ran away instead. Then there was mutual escort, which was two relatively not-crazy patients going places together. And the top, grounds, which meant you could go all over the hospital alone.

Once these stations of the cross were achieved within the hospital, the whole circuit began again in the outside world. Someone who had mutual escort or grounds would probably still be on group outside.

So when we went to Bailey's in Waverley Square with our retinue of nurses, the arrangement of atoms in our molecule was more complex than it appeared to the engineers' wives sipping coffee at the counter and graciously pretending not to look at us.

Lisa wouldn't have been with us. Lisa never made it past one-to-ones after her third escape. Polly was on one-to-ones, but that was to make her feel safe, not hemmed in, and she always came along. Georgina and I were on group, but since nobody else was on group, we were effectively on one-to-twos. Cynthia and the Martian's girlfriend were on one-to-twos; this made it seem that Georgina and I were as crazy as Cynthia and the Martian's girlfriend. We weren't, and there was a bit of resentment on our part. Daisy was at the top of the chart: full towns and grounds. Nobody could understand why.

Six patients, three nurses.

It was a ten- or fifteen-minute walk down the hill, past the rosebushes and stately trees of our beautiful hospital. The farther we got from our ward, the jumpier the nurses became. By the time we hit the street they were silent and closed in on us, and they had assumed the Nonchalant Look, an expression that said, I am not a nurse escorting six lunatics to the ice cream parlor.

But they were, and we were their six lunatics, so we behaved like lunatics.

None of us did anything unusual. We just kept up doing whatever we did back on the ward. Muttering, snarling, crying. Daisy poked people. Georgina complained about not being as crazy as those other two.

"Stop acting out," a nurse would say.

They were not above pinching us or giving a Daisy-like poke to try shutting us up: nurse nips. We didn't blame them for trying, and they didn't blame us for being ourselves. It was all we had—the truth—and the nurses knew it.

Ice Cream

It was a spring day, the sort that gives people hope: all soft winds and delicate smells of warm earth. Suicide weather. Daisy had killed herself the week before. They probably thought we needed distraction. Without Daisy, the staff-to-patient ratio was higher than usual: five patients, three nurses.

Down the hill, past the magnolia already losing its fleshy blossoms, the pink turning brown and rotten along the edge; past the paper-dry daffodils; past the sticky laurel that could crown you or poison you. The nurses were less nervous on the street that day, spring fever making them careless—or perhaps the staff-to-patient ratio was a more comfortable one for them.

The floor of the ice cream parlor bothered me. It was black-and-white checkerboard tile, bigger than supermarket checkerboard. If I looked only at a white square, I would be all right, but it was hard to ignore the black squares that surrounded the white ones. The contrast got under my skin. I always felt itchy in the ice cream parlor. The floor meant Yes, No, This, That, Up, Down, Day, Night—all the indecisions and opposites that were bad enough in life without having them spelled out for you on the floor.

A new boy was dishing out cones. We approached him in a phalanx.

"We want eight ice cream cones," said one of the nurses.

"Okay," he said. He had a friendly, pimply face.

It took a long time to decide what flavors we wanted. It always did.

"Peppermint stick," said the Martian's girlfriend.

"It's just called 'peppermint,' " said Georgina.

"Peppermint dick."

"Honestly." Georgina was revving up for a complaint.

"Peppermint clit."

The Martian's girlfriend got a nurse nip for that.

There were no other takers for peppermint; chocolate was a big favorite. For spring they had a new flavor, peach melba. I ordered that.

"You gonna want nuts on these?" the new boy asked.

We looked at one another: Should we say it? The nurses held their breath. Outside, the birds were singing.

"I don't think we need them," said Georgina.

Checks

Five-minute checks. Fifteen-minute checks. Half-hour checks. Some nurses said, "Checks," when they opened the door. *Click,* turn the knob, *swish,* open the door, "Checks," *swish,* pull the door shut, *click,* turn the knob. Five-minute checks. Not enough time to drink a cup of coffee, read three pages of a book, take a shower.

When digital watches were invented years later they reminded me of five-minute checks. They murdered time in the same way—slowly—chopping off pieces of it and lobbing them into the dustbin with a little click to let you know time was gone. *Click, swish,* "Checks," *swish, click:* another five minutes of life down the drain. And spent in this place.

I got onto half-hour checks eventually, but Georgina remained on fifteen-minute checks, so as long as we were in the same room, it made no difference. *Click, swish,* "Checks," *swish, click.*

It was one reason we preferred sitting in front of the nursing station. The person on checks could pop her head out and take her survey without bothering us.

Sometimes they had the audacity to ask where someone was.

54

Click, swish, "Checks"—the rhythm broke for a moment. "Have you seen Polly?"

"I'm not doing your job for you," Georgina growled.

Swish, click.

Before you knew it, she'd be back. *Click, swish,* "Checks," *swish, click.*

It never stopped, even at night; it was our lullaby. It was our metronome, our pulse. It was our lives measured out in doses slightly larger than those famous coffee spoons. Soup spoons, maybe? Dented tin spoons brimming with what should have been sweet but was sour, gone off, gone by without our savoring it: our lives.

Sharps

Nail scissors. Nail file. Safety razor. Penknife. (The one your father gave you when you were eleven.) Pin. (That pin you got when you graduated from high school, the one with two small pink pearls.) Georgina's gold stud earrings. (You can't be serious! It's the backs, see—the nurse showed her the stubby darts of the backs—they're sharp, see.) That belt. (My belt? What's going on here? The buckle was the culprit. You could maybe put your eye out with this part of the buckle, the pointy part.) Knives. Well, you could make a case for knives. But forks and spoons too? Knives, forks, and spoons.

We ate with plastic. It was a perpetual picnic, our hospital.

Cutting old tough beef with a plastic knife, then scooping it onto a plastic fork (the tines wouldn't stick into the meat, so you had to use the fork like a spoon): Food tastes different eaten with plastic utensils.

One month the plastic-utensil delivery was late and we ate with cardboard knives and forks and spoons. Have you ever eaten with a cardboard fork? Imagine the taste of it, melting clotted cardboard in and out of your mouth, rubbing on your tongue.

How about shaving your legs?

Over to the nursing station. "I want to shave my legs."

"Just a minute."

"I'm going to take a bath now and I want to shave my legs."

"Let me check your orders."

"I've *got* orders to shave my legs. Supervised."

"Let me check." Rustle, rattle. "Okay. Just a minute."

"I'm going now."

In the tub, swimming-pool-sized, Olympic-swimming-pool-sized, deep and long and claw-footed: *Click, swish,* "Checks"—

"Hey! Where's my razor?"

"I'm just the person on checks."

"I'm supposed to shave my legs now."

Swish, click.

More hot water: These hydrotherapy tubs are really comfortable.

Click, swish, my shaving supervisor.

"Did you bring my razor?"

She hands it over. She sits on the chair next to the bathtub. I'm eighteen years old. She's twenty-two. She's watching me shave my legs.

We had a lot of hairy legs on our ward. Early feminists.

Another Lisa

One day a second Lisa arrived. We called her by her full name, Lisa Cody, to distinguish her from the real Lisa, who remained simply Lisa, like a queen.

The Lisas became friends. One of their favorite activities was having phone conversations.

The three phone booths near the double-locked double doors were our only privacy. We could go in one and shut the door. Even the craziest person could sit in a phone booth and have a private conversation—though only with herself. The nurses had lists of permitted numbers for each of us. When we picked up the phone, a nurse would answer.

"Hello," we'd say. "This is Georgina"—or Cynthia, or Polly—"I want to call 555-4270."

"That's not on your list," the nurse would say.

Then the line would go dead.

But there was still the quiet dusty phone booth and the old-fashioned black receiver with its sharp dorsal ridge.

The Lisas had phone conversations. Each one got in a booth, folded the door shut, and yelled into her receiver. When the nurse answered, Lisa yelled, "Off the line!" Then the Lisas got on with their conversation. Sometimes they yelled insults; sometimes they yelled about their plans for the day.

"Wanna go over to the cafeteria for dinner?" Lisa Cody would yell.

But Lisa was restricted to the ward, so she'd have to yell back something like: "Why do you want to eat that slop with all those psychotics?"

To which Lisa Cody would yell, "What do you think you are?"

"Sociopath!" Lisa would yell proudly.

Lisa Cody didn't have a diagnosis yet.

Cynthia was depressive; Polly and Georgina were schizophrenic; I had a character disorder. Sometimes they called it a personality disorder. When I got my diagnosis it didn't sound serious, but after a while it sounded more ominous than other people's. I imagined my character as a plate or shirt that had been manufactured incorrectly and was therefore useless.

When she'd been with us a month or so, Lisa Cody got a diagnosis. She was a sociopath too. She was happy, because she wanted to be like Lisa in all things. Lisa was not so happy, because she had been the only sociopath among us.

"We are very rare," she told me once, "and mostly we are men."

After Lisa Cody got her diagnosis, the Lisas started making more trouble.

"Acting out," the nurses said.

We knew what it was. The real Lisa was proving that Lisa Cody wasn't a sociopath.

Lisa tongued her sleeping meds for a week, took them all at once, and stayed zonked for a day and a night. Lisa Cody managed to save only four of hers, and when she took them, she puked. Lisa put a cigarette out on her arm at six-thirty in the morning while the nurses were changing shifts. That afternoon Lisa Cody burned a tiny welt on her wrist and spent the next twenty minutes running cold water on it.

Then they had a life-history battle. Lisa wormed out of Lisa Cody that she'd grown up in Greenwich, Connecticut.

"Greenwich, Connecticut!" She sneered: No sociopath could emerge from there. "Were you a debutante too?"

Speed, black beauties, coke, heroin—Lisa had done it all. Lisa Cody said she'd been a junkie too. She rolled her sleeve back to show her tracks: faint scratches along the vein as if once, years before, she'd tangled with a rosebush.

"A suburban junkie," said Lisa. "You were playing, that's what."

"Hey, man, junk's junk," Lisa Cody protested.

Lisa pushed her sleeve up to her elbow and shoved her arm under Lisa Cody's nose. Her arm was studded with pale brown lumps, gnarled and authentic.

"These," said Lisa, "are tracks, man. Later for your tracks."

Lisa Cody was beaten, but she didn't have the sense to give up. She still sat beside Lisa at breakfast and Hall Meeting. She still waited in the phone booth for the call that didn't come.

"I gotta get rid of her," said Lisa.

"You're mean," Polly said.

"Fucking bitch," said Lisa.

"Who?" asked Cynthia, Polly's protector.

But Lisa didn't bother to clarify.

One evening when the nurses walked the halls at dusk to turn on the lights that made our ward as bright and jarring as a penny arcade, they found every light bulb gone. Not broken, vanished.

We knew who'd done it. The question was, Where had she put them? It was hard to search in the darkness. Even the light bulbs in our rooms were gone.

"Lisa has the true artistic temperament," said Georgina.

"Just hunt," said the head nurse. "Everybody hunt."

Lisa sat out the hunt in the TV room.

It was Lisa Cody who found them, as she was meant to. She was probably planning to sit out the hunt as well, in the place that held memories of better days. She must have felt some resistance when she tried to fold the door back—there were dozens of light bulbs inside—but she persevered, just as she'd persevered with Lisa. The crunch and clatter brought us all scampering down to the phone booths.

"Broken," said Lisa Cody.

Everyone asked Lisa how she'd done it, but all she would say was, "I've got a long, skinny arm."

Lisa Cody disappeared two days later. Somewhere between our ward and the cafeteria she slipped away. Nobody ever found her, though the search went on for more than a week.

"She couldn't take this place," said Lisa.

And though we listened for a trace of jealousy in her voice, we didn't hear one.

Some months later, Lisa ran off again while she was being taken to a gynecology consult at the Mass. General: two days she managed this time. When she got back, she looked especially pleased with herself.

"I saw Lisa Cody," she said.

"Ooooh," said Georgina. Polly shook her head.

"She's a real junkie now," said Lisa, smiling.

Name: _S. Kaysen._

Date & Time: Nursing Notes

Medication and Treatment Charting:
1. Enter the entire order.
2. Chart every Medicine given and treatment done.

			A.M.		P.M.	

3-11³⁰

While keeping close checks on SK and male visitor (Mr. Hardy) at one point on my round of checks when no more than 5 minutes had gone by I opened the door that was ajar, and observed Mr. Hardy walking away and zipping up his pants, & K. was sitting on the floor. Mr. Hardy left shortly after.

5-25-67

11-7 Slept well ▬▬▬▬

7-3 Multivit + cap P.O. bid   8 ▢   6 ▢

Attended hall meeting. Stated that she found it necessary at times to break ice cubes to get rid of her anger. Watching T.V. and visiting & V.K. ▬▬▬▬

3-11

Quiet earlier in evening; then, upon request showed staff how to make paper flowers. Gradually became more sociable and seemed to be having a good time playing charades the rest of the evening. ▬▬▬▬

Checkmate

We were sitting on the floor in front of the nursing station having a smoke. We liked sitting there. We could keep an eye on the nurses that way.

"On five-minute checks it's impossible," said Georgina.

"I did it," said Lisa Cody.

"Nah," said the real Lisa. "You didn't." She had just started her campaign against Lisa Cody.

"On fifteen, I did it," Lisa Cody amended.

"Maybe on fifteen," said Lisa.

"Oh, fifteen's easy," said Georgina.

"Brad's young," said Lisa. "Fifteen would work."

I hadn't tried yet. Although my boyfriend had calmed down about my being in the hospital and come to visit me, the person on checks caught me giving him a blow job, and we'd been put on supervised visits. He wasn't visiting anymore.

"They caught me," I said. Everybody knew they'd caught me, but I kept mentioning it because it bothered me.

"Big deal," said Lisa. "Fuck them." She laughed. "Fuck *them* and fuck them."

"I don't think he could do it in fifteen minutes," I said.

"No distractions. Right down to business," said Georgina.

65

"Who're you fucking anyhow?" Lisa asked Lisa Cody. Lisa Cody didn't answer. "You're not fucking anybody," said Lisa.

"Fuck you," said Daisy, who was passing by.

"Hey, Daisy," said Lisa, "you ever fuck on five-minute checks?"

"I don't want to fuck these assholes in here," said Daisy.

"Excuses," Lisa whispered.

"You're not fucking anybody either," said Lisa Cody.

Lisa grinned. "Georgina's gonna lend me Brad for an afternoon."

"All it takes is ten minutes," said Georgina.

"They never caught you?" I asked her.

"They don't care. They like Brad."

"You have to fuck patients," Lisa explained. "Get rid of that stupid boyfriend and get a patient boyfriend."

"Yeah, that boyfriend sucks," said Georgina.

"I think he's cute," Lisa Cody said.

"He's trouble," said Lisa.

I started to sniffle.

Georgina patted me. "He doesn't even visit," she pointed out.

"It's true," said Lisa. "He's cute, but he doesn't visit. And where does he get off with that accent?"

"He's English. He grew up in Tunisia." These were very important qualifications for being my boyfriend, I felt.

"Send him back there," Lisa advised.

"I'll take him," said Lisa Cody.

"He can't fuck in fifteen minutes," I warned her. "You'd have to give him a blow job."

"Whatever," said Lisa Cody.

"I like a blow job now and then," said Lisa.

Georgina shook her head. "Too salty."

"I don't mind that," I said.

"Did you ever get one that had a really bitter taste, puckery, like lemons, only worse?" Lisa asked.

"Some kind of dick infection," said Georgina.

"Yuuuch," said Lisa Cody.

"Nah, it's not an infection," said Lisa. "It's just how some of them taste."

"Oh, who needs them," I said.

"We'll find you a new one in the cafeteria," said Georgina.

"Bring a few extra back," said Lisa. She was still restricted to the ward.

"I'm sure Brad knows somebody nice," Georgina went on.

"Let's forget it," I said. The truth was, I didn't want a crazy boyfriend.

Lisa looked at me. "I know what you're thinking," she said. "You don't want some crazy boyfriend, right?"

I was embarrassed and didn't say anything.

"You'll get over it," she told me. "What choice have you got?"

Everybody laughed. Even I had to laugh.

The person on checks put her head out of the nursing station and bobbed it four times, once for each of us.

"Half-hour checks," said Georgina. "That would be good."

"A million dollars would be good, too," said Lisa Cody.

"This place," said Lisa.

We all sighed.

McLean Hospital   F-73

NURSE'S REPORT OF PATIENT ON ADMISSION

Name Kaysen   Sussana   Date 4/27/67

Time Admitted: 1:30 pm   How? Ambulatory ✓   Stretcher   Ward S Bit
                                        (Check One)

Appearance: white female 18 years   Complexion dark
(Note scars, bruises, wounds, etc.)
hair - dk brown   height 5 ft small head - dressed
simple (black & purple) (skirt & sweater) no jewelry, neat, no scars or
distinguishing marks — was wearing Navy P-coat

Behavior: Appeared scared and shy, talked appropriately did
(Active, talkative, depressed, etc.)
cry once during brief encounter c̄ staff member - seemed relaxed
no outward signs of excess nervousness

Temperature: 99²   Pulse: 80   Respiration: 16

Blood Pressure: 118   Height: 60" - 5'   Weight: 96½

Admitting Tub Bath: not given —

Admitting Nurse: ████████████████████ S/N

Remarks by Nurse in Charge: Very depressed, desperate young lady. Quite
tense & cries easily altho tries very hard to maintain composure.
Very cooperative. Talking at gt length of past & present
history.

                        ████████████████ R.N.
                             (Nurse in Charge)

Date: 5/2/67   ████████████████
     (By Supervisor)   (Supervisor)

Do You Believe Him or Me?

That doctor says he interviewed me for three hours. I say it was twenty minutes. Twenty minutes between my walking in the door and his deciding to send me to McLean. I might have spent another hour in his office while he called the hospital, called my parents, called the taxi. An hour and a half is the most I'll grant him.

We can't both be right. Does it matter which of us is right?

It matters to me. But it turns out I'm wrong.

I have a piece of hard evidence, the Time Admitted line from the Nurse's Report of Patient on Admission. From that I can reconstruct everything. It reads: 1:30 P.M.

I said I left home early. But my idea of early might have been as late as nine in the morning. I'd switched night and day—that was one of the things the doctor harped on.

I said I was in his office before eight, but I seem to have been wrong about that, too.

I'll compromise by saying that I left home at eight and spent an hour traveling to a nine o'clock appointment. Twenty minutes later is nine-twenty.

Now let's jump ahead to the taxi ride. The trip from Newton to Belmont takes about half an hour. And I remember waiting fifteen minutes in the Administration Building to sign myself in. Add another fifteen minutes of bureaucracy before I reached the nurse who wrote that report. This totals up to an hour, which means I arrived at the hospital at half past twelve.

And there we are, between nine-twenty and twelve-thirty—a three-hour interview!

I still think I'm right. I'm right about what counts.

But now you believe him.

Don't be so quick. I have more evidence.

The Admission Note, written by the doctor who supervised my case, and who evidently took an extensive history before I reached that nurse. At the top right corner, at the line Hour of Adm., it reads: 11:30 A.M.

Let's reconstruct it again.

Subtracting the half hour waiting to be admitted and wading through bureaucracy takes us to eleven o'clock. Subtracting the half-hour taxi ride takes us to ten-thirty. Subtracting the hour I waited while the doctor made phone calls takes us to nine-thirty. Assuming my departure from home at eight o'clock for a nine o'clock appointment results in a half-hour interview.

There we are, between nine and nine-thirty. I won't quibble over ten minutes.

Now you believe me.

Hospital #22 201   **ADMISSION NOTE**   Hour of Adm: 11:30am

Kaysen, Susanna _____   April 27, 1967   SB II
     NAME OF PATIENT   DATE   HALL

Age: 18   Sex: Female   Marital Status: Single   Religion: Jewish   Occupation: Student ?

Legal Status: Voluntary   Previous Mental   None
                             Hospital Admission:

Accompanied by: Alone

Assigned to: Dr. ████████

Velocity vs. Viscosity

Insanity comes in two basic varieties: slow and fast.

I'm not talking about onset or duration. I mean the quality of the insanity, the day-to-day business of being nuts.

There are a lot of names: depression, catatonia, mania, anxiety, agitation. They don't tell you much.

The predominant quality of the slow form is viscosity.

Experience is thick. Perceptions are thickened and dulled. Time is slow, dripping slowly through the clogged filter of thickened perception. The body temperature is low. The pulse is sluggish. The immune system is half-asleep. The organism is torpid and brackish. Even the reflexes are diminished, as if the lower leg couldn't be bothered to jerk itself out of its stupor when the knee is tapped.

Viscosity occurs on a cellular level. And so does velocity.

In contrast to viscosity's cellular coma, velocity endows every platelet and muscle fiber with a mind of its own, a means of knowing and commenting on its own behavior. There is too much perception, and beyond the plethora of perceptions, a plethora of thoughts about the perceptions and about the fact of having perceptions. Digestion could kill you! What I mean is the unceasing awareness of the processes of digestion could exhaust you to death. And digestion is just an involuntary sideline to thinking, which is where the real trouble begins.

Take a thought—anything; it doesn't matter. I'm tired of sitting here in front of the nursing station: a perfectly reasonable thought. Here's what velocity does to it.

First, break down the sentence: *I'm tired*—well, are you really tired, exactly? Is that like sleepy? You have to check all your body parts for sleepiness, and while you're doing that, there's a bombardment of images of sleepiness, along these lines: head falling onto pillow, head hitting pillow, Wynken, Blynken, and Nod, Little Nemo rubbing sleep from his eyes, a sea monster. Uh-oh, a sea monster. If you're lucky, you can avoid the sea monster and stick with sleepiness. Back to the pillow, memories of having mumps at age five, sensation of swollen cheeks on pillows and pain on salivation—stop. Go back to sleepiness.

But the salivation notion is too alluring, and now there's an excursion into the mouth. You've been here before and it's bad. It's the tongue: Once you think of the tongue it becomes an intrusion. Why is the tongue so large? Why is it scratchy on the sides? Is that a vitamin deficiency? Could you remove the tongue? Wouldn't your mouth be less bothersome without it? There'd be more room in there. The tongue, now, every cell of the tongue, is enormous. It's a vast foreign object in your mouth.

Trying to diminish the size of your tongue, you focus your attention on its components: tip, smooth; back, bumpy; sides, scratchy, as noted earlier (vitamin deficiency); roots—trouble. There are roots to the tongue. You've seen them, and if you put your finger in your mouth you can feel them, but you can't feel them *with* the tongue. It's a paradox.

Paradox. The tortoise and the hare. Achilles and the what? The tortoise? The tendon? The tongue?

Back to tongue. While you weren't thinking of it, it got a little smaller. But thinking of it makes it big again. Why is it scratchy on the sides? Is that a vitamin deficiency? You've thought these thoughts already, but now these thoughts have been stuck onto your tongue. They adhere to the existence of your tongue.

All of that took less than a minute, and there's still the rest of the sentence to figure out. And all you wanted, really, was to decide whether or not to stand up.

Viscosity and velocity are opposites, yet they can look the same. Viscosity causes the stillness of disinclination; velocity causes the stillness of fascination. An observer can't tell if a person is silent and still because inner life has stalled or because inner life is transfixingly busy.

Something common to both is repetitive thought. Experiences seem prerecorded, stylized. Particular patterns of thought get attached to particular movements or activities, and before you know it, it's impossible to approach that movement or activity without dislodging an avalanche of prethought thoughts.

A lethargic avalanche of synthetic thought can take days to fall. Part of the mute paralysis of viscosity comes from knowing every detail of what's ahead and having to wait for its arrival. Here comes the I'm-no-good thought. That takes care of today. All day the insistent dripping of I'm no good. The next thought, the next day, is I'm the Angel of Death.

This thought has a glittering expanse of panic behind it, which is unreachable. Viscosity flattens the effervescence of panic.

These thoughts have no meaning. They are idiot mantras that exist in a prearranged cycle: I'm no good, I'm the Angel of Death, I'm stupid, I can't do anything. Thinking the first thought triggers the whole circuit. It's like the flu: first a sore throat, then, inevitably, a stuffy nose and a cough.

Once, these thoughts must have had a meaning. They must have meant what they said. But repetition has blunted them. They have become background music, a Muzak medley of self-hatred themes.

Which is worse, overload or underload? Luckily, I never had to choose. One or the other would assert itself, rush or dribble through me, and pass on.

Pass on to where? Back into my cells to lurk like a virus waiting for the next opportunity? Out into the ether of the world to wait for the circumstances that would provoke its reappearance? Endogenous or exogenous, nature or nurture—it's the great mystery of mental illness.

Security Screen

"I need some fresh air," said Lisa. We were sitting on the floor in front of the nursing station, as usual.

Daisy passed by.

"Gimme a cigarette," she said.

"Get your own, bitch," said Lisa. Then she gave her one.

"Lousy cigarette," said Daisy. Lisa smoked Kools.

"I need some fresh air," Lisa repeated. She stubbed her cigarette out on the brown-and-beige-speckled rug and stood up. "Hey!" She put her head into the nursing station, in through the open half of the Dutch door. "I need some fucking fresh air."

"Just a minute, Lisa," said a voice from inside.

"Now!" Lisa banged on the sill that divided the top and bottom halves of the door. "This is illegal. You can't keep a person inside a building for months. I'm going to call my lawyer."

Lisa often threatened to call her lawyer. She had a court-appointed lawyer, about twenty-six, handsome, with almond eyes. He hadn't been able to stop her being committed. His name was Irwin. Lisa claimed to have fucked him a few times in the lawyer-client conference room at the courthouse.

Whenever Lisa threatened to call her lawyer, the head nurse got involved.

Now she came out and leaned on the sill. "What's up, Lisa," she said, sounding tired.

"I want some fucking fresh air."

"You don't have to yell," said the head nurse.

"How the fuck else am I going to get any attention in this place?" Lisa always called the hospital "this place."

"I'm right in front of you now," the head nurse said. "I'm paying attention."

"Then you know what I want."

"I'll get an aide to open your window," said the head nurse.

"Window," said Lisa. She turned briefly to look at us. "I'm not interested in some fucking window." She hit the sill again. The head nurse moved back a bit.

"It's window or nothing, Lisa," she said.

"Window or nothing," said Lisa in a singsong. She took a few steps down the hall, so that all of us, including the head nurse, could see her.

"I'd just like to see how you'd manage this place, never going outside, never even *breathing* fresh air, never being able to open your own fucking window, with a bunch of sissy cunts telling you what to do. Valerie, time for lunch, Valerie, you don't have to yell, Valerie, time for your sleeping meds, Valerie, stop acting out. You know? I mean, how the fuck would you manage, hunh?"

The head nurse's name was Valerie.

"I mean, you wouldn't last ten minutes in this place."

"Fucking bitch," said Daisy.

"Who asked you?" Lisa pointed at Daisy.

"Gimme a cigarette," said Daisy.

"Get your own," said Lisa. She turned to the head nurse. "I'm going to call my lawyer."

"Okay," said the head nurse. She was pretty smart.

"You think I've got no rights? Is that what you think?"

"Should I put the call through?"

Lisa waved her arm dismissively. "Nah," she said. "Nah, open the window."

"Judy," said the head nurse. This was a young blond aide we enjoyed tormenting.

"Valerie!" yelled Lisa. She called the head nurse Valerie only when she was upset. "Valerie, I want *you* to open my window."

"I'm busy, Lisa."

"I'll call my lawyer."

"Judy can do it."

"I don't want that fucking sissy cunt in my room."

"Oh, you're such a bore," said the head nurse. She pressed the security buzzer that unlocked the bottom of the door and came out into the hall with us.

Lisa smiled.

To open a window, a staff person had to unlock the security screen, which was a thick impregnable mesh on a steel frame, then lift the heavy unbreakable-glass-paned window, then shut and relock the security screen. This took about three minutes, and it was hard work. It was the sort of thing aides did. When the window was open, air might make its way through the mesh of the security screen, if it was a breezy day.

The head nurse returned from Lisa's room, a little pink from exertion. "Okay," she said. She rapped on the nursing-station door to be buzzed back in.

Lisa lit another cigarette.

"Your window's open," said the head nurse.

"I'm aware of that," said Lisa.

"You aren't even going in there, are you?" The head nurse sighed.

"Hey, man," said Lisa, "it passes the time." She touched the hot end of her cigarette to her arm for a second. "I mean, that took up twenty minutes, maybe half an hour."

The buzzer sounded, the head nurse opened the door, went inside, and leaned on the sill again.

"Yes, it does pass the time," she said.

"Gimme a cigarette," said Daisy.

"Get your own, bitch," said Lisa. Then she gave her one.

Keepers

Valerie was about thirty. She was tall and had tapered legs and arms. She looked a lot like Lisa, though she was fair. They both had lean long haunches and flexible joints. Lisa was good at curling herself into chairs and corners, and so was Valerie. When someone was upset and had tucked herself between a radiator and a wall or behind a bathtub or into another small secure spot, Valerie could curl herself into a compact package and sit near that person.

Valerie's fair hair was beautiful, but she kept it hidden in a braid that she twisted up on the back of her head. This braid-in-a-bun never came undone or slipped out of place. Rarely, Valerie could be coaxed into undoing the bun and showing us the braid, which reached to her waist. Only Lisa could convince her to do this. She never released her hair from the braid, though we begged her to.

Valerie was strict and inflexible and she was the only staff person we trusted. We trusted her because she wasn't afraid of us. She wasn't afraid of doctors either. She didn't have much to say about anything, and we liked her for that, too.

We had to hear a lot of talk in that place. Each of us saw three doctors a day: the ward doctor, the resident, and our own therapist. Mostly we had to hear ourselves talk to these doctors, but they did a fair amount of talking themselves.

They had a special language: *regression, acting out, hostility, withdrawal, indulging in behavior.* This last phrase could be attached to any activity and make it sound suspicious: indulging in eating behavior, talking behavior, writing behavior. In the outside world people ate and talked and wrote, but nothing we did was simple.

Valerie was a relief from that. The only phrase she used was *acting out,* and she used it correctly, to mean "getting in my hair and driving me crazy." She said things like "Cut that out" and "You're a bore." She said what she meant, just as we did.

The doctors were men; the nurses and aides were women. There were two exceptions: Jerry the Aide and Dr. Wick. Jerry was willowy and worried. He had one good trick. Now and then, someone with a lot of privileges was allowed to leave the hospital in a taxi. That person would say, "Jerry, call me a cab." Jerry would say, "You're a cab." We loved this.

Dr. Wick was another story.

Dr. Wick was the head of our ward, South Belknap Two. The wards had boarding-school names like East House and South Belknap, and Dr. Wick would have been a good boarding-school matron. She came from Rhodesia and she looked like the ghost of a horse. When she talked, she sounded somewhat like a horse as well. She had a low, burbly voice, and her colonial English accent gave her sentences a neighing cadence.

Dr. Wick seemed utterly innocent about American culture, which made her an odd choice to head an adolescent girls' ward. And she was easily shocked about sexual matters. The word *fuck* made her pale horse face flush; it flushed a lot when she was around us.

A representative conversation with Dr. Wick:

"Good morning. It has been decided that you were compulsively promiscuous. Would you like to tell me about that?"

"No." This is the best of several bad responses, I've decided.

"For instance, the attachment to your high school English teacher." Dr. Wick always uses words like *attachment*.

"Uh?"

"Would you like to tell me about that?"

"Um. Well. He drove me to New York." That was when I realized he was interested. He brought along a wonderful vegetarian lunch for me. "But that wasn't when it was."

"What? When what was?"

"When we fucked."

(Flush.) "Go on."

"We went to the Frick. I'd never been there. There was this Vermeer, see, this amazing painting of a girl having a music lesson—I just couldn't believe how amazing it was—"

"So when did you—ah—when was it?"

Doesn't she want to hear about the Vermeer? That's what I remember. "What?"

"The—ah—attachment. How did it start?"

"Oh, later, back home." Suddenly I know what she wants. "I was at his house. We had poetry meetings at his house. And everybody had left, so we were just sitting there on the sofa alone. And he said, 'Do you want to fuck?' "

(Flush.) "He used that word?"

"Yup." He didn't. He kissed me. And he'd kissed me in New York too. But why should I disappoint her?

This was called therapy.

Luckily, Dr. Wick had a lot of girls to take care of, so therapy with her was brief, maybe five minutes a day. But in her wake came the resident.

There was a two- or three-minute breather between Dr. Wick's departure and the resident's arrival. During this time we could think of new things to say or formulate complaints. Residents were in charge of privileges, medication, phone calls—the day-to-day matters that were not important enough for Dr. Wick to bother with.

Residents changed every six months. We'd just begin to figure out how to manage one resident when he'd be snatched out from under us and replaced with a new, incomprehensible resident. They started out tough and ended up exhausted and ready to leave. A few started out with compassion; they ended up bitter, because we took advantage of them.

A representative conversation with a resident:

"Good morning. How are your bowel movements?"

"I want to get off group. I want destination privileges."

"Do you have any headaches?"

"I've been on group for six months!"

"The head nurse said you were acting out after lunch yesterday."

"She's making that up."

"Hmmmm. Hostility." He scribbles in a notebook.

"Can I have orders for Tylenol instead of aspirin?"

"There's no difference."

"Aspirin gives me a stomach ache."

"Are you having headaches?"

"This is in case I do."

"Hmmmm. Hypochondria." He scribbles again.

But these two doctors were hors d'oeuvres. The entrée was the therapist.

Most of us saw our therapists every day. Cynthia didn't; she had therapy twice a week and shock therapy once a week. And Lisa didn't go to therapy. She had a therapist, but he used her hour to take a nap. If she was extremely bored, she'd demand to be taken to his office, where she'd find him snoozing in his chair. "Gotcha!" she'd say. Then she'd come back to the ward. The rest of us traipsed off day after day to exhume the past.

Therapists had nothing to do with our everyday lives.

"Don't talk about the hospital," my therapist said if I complained about Daisy or a stupid nurse. "We're not here to talk about the hospital."

They couldn't grant or rescind privileges, help us get rid of smelly roommates, stop aides from pestering us. The only power they had was the power to dope us up. Thorazine, Stelazine, Mellaril, Librium, Valium: the therapists' friends. The resident could put us on that stuff too, in an "acute" situation. Once we were on it, it was hard to get off. A bit like heroin, except it was the staff who got addicted to our taking it.

"You're doing so well," the resident would say.

That was because those things knocked the heart out of us.

Half a dozen nurses, including Valerie, and an aide or two were on duty during the day. The night staff consisted of three comfy big-bosomed Irish women who called us "dearie." Occasionally there was a comfy big-bosomed black woman who called us "honey." The night staff would hug us if we needed a hug. The day staff adhered to the No Physical Contact rule.

Between day and night was a dark universe called evening, which began at three-fifteen, when the day staff retired to the living room to gossip about us with the evening staff. At three-thirty everyone emerged. Power had been transferred. From then until eleven, when the comfy women took over, we were in Mrs. McWeeney's hands.

Perhaps it was Mrs. McWeeney who made dusk such a dangerous time. No matter the season, dusk began at three-fifteen with her arrival.

Mrs. McWeeney was dry, tight, small, and pig-eyed. If Dr. Wick was a disguised boarding-school matron, Mrs. McWeeney was an undisguised prison matron. She had hard gray hair pressed into waves that grasped her scalp like a migraine. The day nurses, following Valerie's lead, wore unbuttoned nurse coats over street clothes. No such informality for Mrs. McWeeney. She wore a creaky white uniform and spongy ripple-soled nurse shoes that she painted white every week; we could watch the paint cracking and peeling off between Monday and Friday.

Mrs. McWeeney and Valerie did not get along. This was fascinating, like overhearing your parents having a fight. Mrs. McWeeney cast on Valerie's clothes and hair the same disapproving eye she gave us and clicked her teeth with impatience as Valerie gathered her coat and pocketbook and left the nursing station at three-thirty. Valerie ignored her. Valerie was able to ignore people in an obvious way.

As long as Valerie was on the ward, we felt safe hating Mrs. McWeeney. But as soon as her long tapered back had receded down the hall and out the double-locked double doors, we were overcome by gloom shot through with anxiety: Now Mrs. McWeeney was in power.

Her power wasn't absolute, but it was close. She shared it with a mysterious Doctor on Call. She never called him. "I can handle this," she said.

She had more confidence in her ability to handle things than we did. Many evenings were spent arguing about whether the Doctor on Call should make an appearance.

"We'll just have to agree to disagree," Mrs. McWeeney said about ten times per evening. She had an endless store of clichés.

When Mrs. McWeeney said, "We'll just have to agree to disagree" or "Little pitchers have big ears" or "Smile and the world smiles with you, cry and you cry alone," a faint but delighted grin came onto her face.

Clearly, she was nuts. We were locked up for eight hours a day with a crazy woman who hated us.

Mrs. McWeeney was unpredictable. She'd gnarl her face up for no reason while giving out bedtime meds and slam back into the nursing station without a word. We'd have to wait for her to calm down before getting our nightly Mickey Finns; sometimes we waited as long as half an hour.

Every morning we complained to Valerie about Mrs. McWeeney, though we never said anything about waiting for our meds. We knew Mrs. McWeeney was a crazy person who had to earn a living. We weren't trying to get her decertified, we just wanted her off our ward.

Valerie was unsympathetic to our complaints.

"Mrs. McWeeney is a professional," she said. "She's been in this business a lot longer than I have."

"So what?" said Georgina.

"She's fucking nuts," Lisa yelled.

"You don't have to yell, Lisa—I'm right here," said Valerie.

We were all protecting Mrs. McWeeney, one way or another.

Mrs. McWeeney wasn't the only person in need of protection.

Now and then there was an influx of student nurses. They were migratory, passing through our hospital on their way to operating rooms and cardiac-care units. They followed real nurses around in a flock, asking questions and getting underfoot. "Oh, that Tiffany! She sticks to me like a barnacle," the nurses would complain. Then we got the chance to say, "Sucks, doesn't it? Being followed around all the time." The nurses would have to grant us this point.

The student nurses were about nineteen or twenty: our age. They had clean, eager faces and clean, ironed uniforms. Their innocence and incompetence aroused our pity, unlike the incompetence of aides, which aroused our scorn. This was partly because student nurses stayed only a few weeks, whereas aides were incompetent for years at a stretch. Mainly, though, it was because when we looked at the student nurses, we saw alternate versions of ourselves. They were living out lives we might have been living, if we hadn't been occupied with being mental patients. They shared apartments and had boyfriends and talked about clothes. We wanted to protect them so that they could go on living these lives. They were our proxies.

They loved talking to us. We asked them what movies they'd seen and how they'd done on their exams and when they were getting married (most of them had sadly small engagement rings). They'd tell us anything—that the boyfriend was insisting they "do it" before the wedding, that the mother was a drinker, that the grades were bad and the scholarship wasn't going to be renewed.

We gave them good advice. "Use a condom"; "Call Alcoholics Anonymous"; "Work hard for the rest of the semester and bring your grades up." Later they'd report back to us: "You were right. Thanks a lot."

We did our best to control our snarls and mutterings and tears when they were around. Consequently, they learned nothing about psychiatric nursing. When they finished their rotation, all they took with them were improved versions of us, halfway between our miserable selves and the normality we saw embodied in them.

For some of us, this was the closest we would ever come to a cure.

As soon as they left, things went quickly back to worse than usual, and the real nurses had their hands full.

Thus, our keepers. As for finders—well, we had to be our own finders.

Nineteen Sixty-Eight

The world didn't stop because we weren't in it anymore, far from it. Night after night tiny bodies fell to the ground on our TV screen: black people, young people, Vietnamese people, poor people—some dead, some only bashed up for the moment. There were always more of them to replace the fallen and join them the next night.

Then came the period when people we knew—not knew personally, but knew of—started falling to the ground: Martin Luther King, Robert Kennedy. Was that more alarming? Lisa said it was natural. "They gotta kill them," she explained. "Otherwise it'll never settle down."

But it didn't seem to be settling down. People were doing the kinds of things we had fantasies of doing: taking over universities and abolishing classes; making houses out of cardboard boxes and putting them in people's way; sticking their tongues out at policemen.

We'd cheer them on, those little people on our TV screen, who shrank as their numbers increased until they were just a mass of dots taking over universities and sticking their tiny tongues out. We thought eventually they'd get around to "liberating" us too. "Right on!" we'd yell at them.

Fantasies don't include repercussions. We were safe in our

expensive, well-appointed hospital, locked up with our rages and rebellions. Easy for us to say "Right on!" The worst we got was an afternoon in seclusion. Usually all we got was a smile, a shake of the head, a note on our charts: "Identification with protest movement." They got cracked skulls, black eyes, kicks to the kidneys—and then, they got locked up with their rages and rebellions.

So it went on, month after month of battles and riots and marches. These were easy times for the staff. We didn't "act out"; it was all acted out for us.

We were not only calm, we were expectant. The world was about to flip, the meek were about to inherit the earth or, more precisely, wrest it from the strong, and we, the meekest and weakest, would be heirs to the vast estate of all that had been denied us.

But this didn't happen—not for us and not for any of those other claimants to the estate.

It was when we saw Bobby Seale bound and gagged in a Chicago courtroom that we realized the world wasn't going to change. He was in chains like a slave.

Cynthia was particularly upset. "They do that to me!" she cried. It was true that they did tie you down and put something in your mouth when you had shock, to stop you from biting your tongue during the convulsion.

Lisa was angry too, but for another reason. "Don't you see the difference?" she snarled at Cynthia. "They have to gag him, because they're afraid people will believe what he says."

We looked at him, a tiny dark man in chains on our TV screen with the one thing we would always lack: credibility.

93

Bare Bones

For many of us, the hospital was as much a refuge as it was a prison. Though we were cut off from the world and all the trouble we enjoyed stirring up out there, we were also cut off from the demands and expectations that had driven us crazy. What could be expected of us now that we were stowed away in a loony bin?

The hospital shielded us from all sorts of things. We'd tell the staff to refuse phone calls or visits from anyone we didn't want to talk to, including our parents.

"I'm too upset!" we'd wail, and we wouldn't have to talk to whoever it was.

As long as we were willing to be upset, we didn't have to get jobs or go to school. We could weasel out of anything except eating and taking our medication.

In a strange way we were free. We'd reached the end of the line. We had nothing more to lose. Our privacy, our liberty, our dignity: All of this was gone and we were stripped down to the bare bones of our selves.

Naked, we needed protection, and the hospital protected us. Of course, the hospital had stripped us naked in the first place—but that just underscored its obligation to shelter us.

And the hospital fulfilled its obligation. Somebody in our

families had to pay a good deal of money for that: sixty dollars (1967 dollars) a day just for the room; therapy, drugs, and
consultations were extra. Ninety days was the usual length of
mental-hospital insurance coverage, but ninety days was
barely enough to get started on a visit to McLean. My workup
alone took ninety days. The price of several of those college
educations I didn't want was spent on my hospitalization.

If our families stopped paying, we stopped staying and
were put naked into a world we didn't know how to live in
anymore. Writing a check, dialing a telephone, opening a
window, locking a door—these were just a few of the things
we all forgot how to do.

Our families. The prevailing wisdom was that they were
the reason we were in there, yet they were utterly absent
from our hospital lives. We wondered: Were we as absent
from their lives outside?

Lunatics are similar to designated hitters. Often an entire
family is crazy, but since an entire family can't go into the
hospital, one person is designated as crazy and goes inside.
Then, depending on how the rest of the family is feeling,
that person is kept inside or snatched out, to prove something about the family's mental health.

Most families were proving the same proposition: *We
aren't crazy; she* is the crazy one. Those families kept paying.

But some families had to prove that nobody was crazy,
and they were the ones who threatened to stop paying.

Torrey had that sort of a family.

We all liked Torrey, because she had a noble bearing.
The only thing wrong with her was amphetamines. She'd
spent two years shooting speed in Mexico, where her family

lived. Amphetamines had made her face pale and her voice tired and drawling—or, rather, it was the lack of amphetamines that made her this way.

Torrey was the only person Lisa respected, probably because they had the needle in common.

Every few months Torrey's parents flew from Mexico to Boston to harangue her. She was crazy, she had driven them crazy, she was malingering, they couldn't afford it, and so forth. After they left Torrey would give a report in her tired drawl.

"Then Mom said, 'You made me into an alcoholic,' and then Dad said, 'I'm going to see you never get out of this place,' and then they sort of switched and Mom said, 'You're nothing but a junkie,' and Dad said, 'I'm not going to pay for you to take it easy in here while we suffer.'"

"Why do you see them?" Georgina asked.

"Oh," said Torrey.

"It's how they show their love," said Lisa. Her parents never made contact with her.

The nurses agreed with Lisa. They told Torrey she was mature for agreeing to see her parents when she knew they were going to confuse her. *Confuse* was the nurses' word for *abuse*.

Torrey was not confused. "I don't mind this place," she said. "It's a break from Mexico." In Torrey's mouth, *Mexico* sounded like a curse.

"Mexico," she'd say, and shake her head.

In Mexico there was a big house with porches back and front, there were servants, there was sun every day, and there were amphetamines for sale in the drugstore.

Lisa thought it sounded pretty good.

"It's death," said Torrey. "Being in Mexico means being dead and shooting speed to feel like you're not quite dead. That's all."

Sometimes Valerie or another nurse tried explaining to Torrey that she could be in Mexico without going to the drugstore and buying amphetamines.

"You haven't been there," Torrey said.

In August Torrey's parents called to announce that they were coming up to get her.

"Taking me home to die," she said.

"We won't let you go," said Georgina.

"That's right," I said. "Right, Lisa?"

Lisa wasn't making any promises. "What can we do about it?"

"Nothing," said Torrey.

That afternoon I asked Valerie, "You wouldn't let Torrey's parents take her back to Mexico, would you?"

"We're here to protect you," she said.

"What does that mean?" I asked Lisa that evening.

"Doesn't mean shit," said Lisa.

For about a week there was no word from Torrey's parents. Then they called to say they'd meet her at the Boston airport. They didn't want to bother with coming out to the hospital to pick her up.

"You could hop out on the way to the airport," said Lisa. "Somewhere downtown. Get right onto the subway." She was an old hand at escape planning.

"I don't have any money," said Torrey.

We pooled our money. Georgina had twenty-two dollars; Polly had eighteen; Lisa had twelve; I had fifteen ninety-five.

"You could live for weeks on this," Lisa told her.

"One, maybe," said Torrey. But she looked less depressed. She took the money and put it in her bra. It made quite a lump. "Thanks," she said.

"You've got to have a plan," Lisa said. "Are you going to stay here or leave town? I think you ought to leave town right away."

"And go where?"

"Don't you have any friends in New York?" Georgina asked.

Torrey shook her head. "I know you people, and I know some junkies in Mexico. That's it."

"Lisa Cody," said Lisa. "She's a junkie. She'd put you up."

"She's not reliable," said Georgina.

"She'd use all that money for junk anyhow," I said.

"I might too," Torrey pointed out.

"That's different," said Lisa. "We gave it to you."

"Don't," said Polly. "You might as well go back to Mexico if you do that."

"Yeah," said Torrey. Now she looked depressed again.

"What's up?" said Lisa.

"I don't have the nerve," said Torrey. "I can't do it."

"Yes, you can," said Lisa. "You just open the door at a red light and tear off. You just get the fuck away. You can do it."

"You could do it," said Torrey. "I can't."

"You've got to do it," said Georgina.

"I know you can do it," Polly said. She put her pink-and-white hand on Torrey's thin shoulder.

I wondered if Torrey could do it.

In the morning, two nurses were waiting to take Torrey to the airport.

"That's not going to work," Lisa whispered to me. "She'll never get away from two."

She decided to create a diversion. The point was to occupy enough staff members so that only one nurse would be available to take Torrey to the airport.

"This fucking place!" Lisa yelled. She went down the hall slamming the doors to the rooms. "Eat shit!"

It worked. Valerie shut the top of the Dutch door to the nursing station and had a powwow with the rest of the staff while Lisa yelled and slammed. When they emerged, they fanned out in trouble-shooting formation.

"Calm down, Lisa," said Valerie. "Where's Torrey? It's time to go. Let's go."

Lisa paused on her circuit. "Are you taking her?"

We all knew nobody could escape from Valerie.

Valerie shook her head. "No. Now calm down, Lisa."

Lisa slammed another door.

"It's not going to help," Valerie said. "It's not going to stop anything."

"Valerie, you promised—" I began.

"Where's Torrey?" Valerie interrupted me. "Let's just get this over with."

"I'm here," said Torrey. She was holding a suitcase, and her arm was trembling, so the suitcase was bumping against her leg.

"Okay," said Valerie. She reached into the nursing station and pulled out a full medication cup. "Take this," she said.

"What the fuck is that?" yelled Lisa from halfway down the hall.

"It'll just relax Torrey," Valerie said. "Something to relax her."

"I'm relaxed," said Torrey.

"Drink up," said Valerie.

"Don't take it!" Lisa yelled. "Don't do it, Torrey!"

Torrey tipped her head back and drank.

"Thank God," Valerie muttered. "Okay. All right. This is it." She was shaking too. "Okay. Good-bye, Torrey dear, good-bye now."

Torrey was actually leaving. She was going to get on the airplane and go back to Mexico.

Lisa quit banging and came up to stand with the rest of us. We stood around the nursing station looking at Torrey.

"Was that what I think it was?" Lisa asked Valerie. She put her face up to Valerie's face. "Was that Thorazine? Is that what that was?"

Valerie didn't answer. She didn't need to. Torrey's eyes were already glistening. She took a step away from us and lost her balance slightly. Valerie caught her elbow.

"It's all right," she told Torrey.

"I know," said Torrey. She cleared her throat. "Sure."

The nurse who was taking her to the airport picked up the suitcase and led Torrey down the hall to the double-locked double doors.

Then there wasn't anything to do. An aide went into Torrey's room and started stripping the sheets off the bed.

Valerie went back inside the nursing station. Lisa slammed a door. The rest of us stood where we were for a while. Then we watched TV until the nurse came back from the airport. We fell silent, listening for agitation in the nursing station— the sort of agitation an escape provokes. But nothing happened.

The day got worse after that. It didn't matter where we were; every place was the wrong place. The TV room was too hot; the living room was too weird; the floor in front of the nursing station was no good either. Georgina and I tried sitting in our room, and that was terrible as well. Every room was echoey and big and empty. And there was just nothing to do.

Lunch came: tuna melt. Who wanted it? We hated tuna melt.

After lunch Polly said, "Let's just plan to spend one hour in the living room and then one hour in front of the nursing station and so on. At least it will be a schedule."

Lisa wasn't interested. But Georgina and I agreed to give it a whirl.

We started in the living room. Each of us plopped into a yellow vinyl chair. Two o'clock on a Saturday in August on a medium-security ward in Belmont. Old cigarette smoke, old magazines, green spotted rug, five yellow vinyl chairs, a broken-backed orange sofa: You couldn't mistake that room for anything but a loony-bin living room.

I sat in my yellow vinyl chair not thinking about Torrey. Instead, I looked at my hand. It occurred to me that my palm looked like a monkey's palm. The crinkle of the three lines running across it and the way my fingers curled in seemed simian to me. If I spread my fingers out, my hand looked more human, so I did that. But it was tiring holding my fingers apart. I let them relax, and then the monkey idea came back.

I turned my hand over quickly. The back of it wasn't much better. My veins bulged—maybe because it was such a hot day—and the skin around my knuckles was wrinkly and loose. If I moved my hand I could see the three long bones that stretched out from the wrist to the first joints of my fingers. Or perhaps those weren't bones but tendons? I poked one; it was resilient, so probably it was a tendon. Underneath, though, were bones. At least I hoped so.

I poked deeper, to feel the bones. They were hard to find. Knucklebones were easy, but I wanted to find the hand bones, the long ones going from my wrist to my fingers.

I started getting worried. Where were my bones? I put my hand in my mouth and bit it, to see if I crunched down on something hard. Everything slid away from me. There were nerves; there were blood vessels; there were tendons: All these things were slippery and elusive.

"Damn," I said.

Georgina and Polly weren't paying attention.

I began scratching at the back of my hand. My plan was to get hold of a flap of skin and peel it away, just to have a look. I wanted to see that my hand was a normal human hand, with bones. My hand got red and white—sort of like Polly's hands—but I couldn't get my skin to open up and let me in.

I put my hand in my mouth and chomped. Success! A bubble of blood came out near my last knuckle, where my incisor had pierced the skin.

"What the fuck are you doing?" Georgina asked.

"I'm trying to get to the bottom of this," I said.

"Bottom of what?" Georgina looked angry.

"My hand," I said, waving it around. A dribble of blood went down my wrist.

"Well, stop it," she said.

"It's my hand," I said. I was angry too. And I was getting really nervous. Oh God, I thought, there aren't any bones in there, there's nothing in there.

"Do I have any bones?" I asked them. "Do I have any bones? Do you think I have any bones?" I couldn't stop asking.

"Everybody has bones," said Polly.

"But do *I* have any bones?"

"You've got them," said Georgina. Then she ran out of the room. She came back in half a minute with Valerie.

"Look at her," Georgina said, pointing at me.

Valerie looked at me and went away.

"I just want to see them," I said. "I just have to be sure."

"They're in there—I promise you," said Georgina.

"I'm not safe," I said suddenly.

Valerie was back, with a full medication cup.

"Valerie, I'm not safe," I said.

"You take this." She gave me the cup.

I could tell it was Thorazine from the color. I'd never had it before. I tipped my head back and drank.

It was sticky and sour and it oozed into my stomach. The taste of it stayed in my throat. I swallowed a few times.

"Oh, Valerie," I said, "you promised—" Then the Thorazine hit me. It was like a wall of water, strong but soft.

"Wow," I said. I couldn't hear my own voice very well. I decided to stand up, but when I did, I found myself on the floor.

Valerie and Georgina picked me up under the arms and steered me down the hall to our room. My legs and feet felt like mattresses, they were so huge and dense. Valerie and Georgina felt like mattresses too, big soft mattresses pressing on either side of me. It was comforting.

"It'll be okay, won't it?" I asked. My voice was far away from me and I hadn't said what I meant. What I meant was that now I was safe, now I was really crazy, and nobody could take me out of there.

1967
Aug. 9

PROGRESS NOTE   The patient has been doing extremely well aside from
depressive reactions on the weekend, until yesterday,
when she was listening to some records and suddenly felt as though she were
a teenager again and began to become very frightened at the thought that she
had never had a satisfactory childhood. She became fearful and agitated
requiring a call from the doctor on call. She expressed her fears regarding
her parents and lack of communication, the fact that she has been unable to
make satisfactory decisions throughout her life to the present time, and also,
that her therapist is away. She is extremely agitated today and, although
not disorganized, she is going to need further support in helping her get
through the time that her therapist is away. She is most extremely upset
about her parents and their lack of understanding and she relates this to
other people, and that they can't understand or can't be trusted. I have
spoken to her at length about decision-making and responsibility and she
does feel better after venting some of these feelings.   However, she will
also have to be somewhat supported and protected, at the present time, as she
is going through a rather trying time without her therapist.

8/24/67

PROGRESS NOTE: The patient suffered an episode of depersonalization
on Saturday for about six hours at which time she felt
that she wasn't a real person, nothing but skin. She talked about
wanting to cut herself to see whether she would bleed to prove to herself that she was a real person. She mentioned she would like to see
an X-ray of herself to see if she has any bones or anything inside.
The precipitating event for this episode of depersonalization is still
not clear.

Dental Health

I was sitting in the cafeteria eating meat loaf when some-thing peculiar happened inside my jaw. My cheek started swelling up. By the time I got back to the ward I had a Ping-Pong ball on the side of my face.

"Wisdom tooth," said Valerie.

We went over to see the dentist.

His office was in the Administration Building, where long ago I'd sat quietly waiting to be locked up. The dentist was tall, sullen, and dirty, with speckles of blood on his lab coat and a pubic mustache. When he put his fingers in my mouth they tasted of ear wax.

"Abscess," he said. "I'll take it right out."

"No," I said.

"No what?" He was shuffling through his tool tray.

"I won't." I looked at Valerie. "I won't let you."

Valerie looked out the window. "Could control it with some antibiotics for the moment," she said.

"Could," he said. He looked at me. I bared the rest of my teeth at him. "Okay," he said.

On our way back Valerie said, "That was sensible of you."

It had been a long time since I'd heard myself called

anything as complimentary as *sensible*. "That guy looked like a pimple," I said.

"Have to get the infection under control first," Valerie muttered to herself as she unlocked the double doors to our ward.

The first day of penicillin the Ping-Pong ball turned into a marble. By the second day the marble had turned into a pea, but there was a rash on my face. Also I was too hot.

"No postponing it now," said Valerie. "And don't take penicillin again, ever."

"I won't go," I said.

"I'm taking you to my dentist in Boston tomorrow," she said.

Everybody was excited. "Boston!" Polly wiggled her striped hands. "What are you going to wear?" "You could go to a matinee," said Georgina, "and eat popcorn." "You could score something for me," said Lisa. "Down near Jordan Marsh there's this guy with a blue baseball cap—" "You could jump out at a red light and split," said Cynthia. "His name is Astro," Lisa continued. She was more realistic than Cynthia; she knew I wouldn't split. "He sells black beauties cheap."

"I look like a chipmunk," I said. "I can't do anything."

In the cab I was too nervous to look at Boston.

"Lean back and count to ten," said the dentist. Before I got to four I was sitting up with a hole in my mouth.

"Where did it go?" I asked him.

He held up my tooth, huge, bloody, spiked, and wrinkled.

But I'd been asking about the time. I was ahead of myself. He'd dropped me into the future, and I didn't know what had happened to the time in between. "How long did that take?" I asked.

"Oh, nothing," he said. "In and out."

That didn't help. "Like five seconds? Like two minutes?"

He moved away from the chair. "Valerie," he called.

"I need to know," I said.

"No hot liquids for twenty-four hours," he said.

"How long?"

"Twenty-four hours."

Valerie came in, all business. "Up you get, let's go."

"I need to know how long that took," I said, "and he won't tell me."

She gave me one of her withering looks. "Not long, I can tell you that."

"It's my time!" I yelled. "It's my time and I need to know how much it was."

The dentist rolled his eyes. "I'll let you handle this," he said, and left the room.

"Come on," said Valerie. "Don't make trouble for me."

"Okay." I got out of the dentist's chair. "I'm not making trouble for *you*, anyhow."

In the cab Valerie said, "I've got something for you."

It was my tooth, cleaned up a bit but huge and foreign.

"I snitched it for you," she said.

"Thanks, Valerie, that was nice of you." But the tooth wasn't what I really wanted. "I want to know how much time that was," I said. "See, Valerie, I've lost some time, and I need to know how much. I need to know."

Then I started crying. I didn't want to, but I couldn't help it.

Calais Is Engraved on My Heart

A new name had appeared on the blackboard: Alice Calais.

"Let's guess about her," said Georgina.

"Some new nut," said Lisa.

"When is she coming?" I asked Valerie.

Valerie pointed down the hall toward the doors. And there she was, Alice Calais.

She was young, like us, and she didn't look too crazy. We got up off the floor to say hello properly.

"I'm Alice Calais," she said, but she said *callous*.

"Cal-lay?" said Georgina.

Alice Calais-Callous squinted. "Hunh?"

"You say it *callous*," I told Georgina. I thought she was rude to imply that Alice didn't know how to say her own name.

"Cal-lay?" Georgina said again.

Valerie came over at that point to show Alice her room.

"It's like Vermont," I said to Georgina. "We don't say *Vayr-mon* like the French do."

"Phonetics," said Lisa.

Alice Calais-Callous was timid, but she liked us. She often sat near us and listened. Lisa thought she was a bore. Georgina tried to draw her out.

"You know, that's a French name," she told Alice. "Calais."

"Callous," said Alice. "It is?"

"Yes. It's a place in France. A famous place."

"Why?"

"It used to belong to England," said Georgina. "A lot of France did. Then they lost it in the Hundred Years' War. Calais was the last place they lost."

"A hundred years!" Alice widened her eyes.

It was easy to impress Alice. She knew almost nothing about anything. Lisa thought she was a retard.

One morning we were sitting in the kitchen eating toast with honey.

"What's that?" asked Alice.

"Toast with honey."

"I've never had honey," Alice said.

This was stunning. Who could imagine a life so circumscribed that it excluded honey?

"Never?" I asked.

Georgina passed her a piece. We watched while she ate.

"It tastes like bees," she announced.

"What do you mean?" Lisa asked.

"Sort of furry and tingly—like bees."

I took another bite of my toast. The honey just tasted like honey, something I couldn't remember tasting for the first time.

Later that day, when Alice was off having a Rorschach, I asked, "How can a person who's never eaten honey have a family that can afford to send her here?"

"Probably really incredibly crazy and interesting, so they let her in for less," said Georgina.

"I doubt it," said Lisa.

And for several weeks Alice Calais-Callous gave no evidence of being either really crazy or interesting. Even Georgina got tired of her.

"She doesn't know anything," said Georgina. "It's as if she spent her life in a closet."

"She probably did," said Lisa. "Locked up in a closet eating Cheerios."

"You mean kept there by her parents?" I asked.

"Why not," said Lisa. "After all, they named her Alice Callous."

It was as good an explanation as any for why, after about a month, Alice exploded like a volcano.

"Lot of energy in that girl," Georgina observed. Down at the end of the hall, muffled booming and yelling and crashing came out of the seclusion room.

The next day as we sat on the floor under the blackboard Alice was marched past us between two nurses on her way to maximum security. Her face was puffy from crying and bashing around. She didn't look at us. She was occupied by her own complicated thoughts—you could tell from the way she was squinting and moving her mouth.

Her name came off the blackboard rather quickly.

"Guess she's settled in over there," said Lisa.

"We ought to go see her," said Georgina.

The nurses thought it was nice that we wanted to visit Alice. It was even all right for Lisa to go. They must have figured she couldn't get into trouble on maximum security.

It didn't look special from the outside. It didn't even have extra doors. But inside it was different. The windows had screens like our windows, but there were bars in front of the screens. Little bars, thin and several inches apart; still, they were bars. The bathrooms had no doors, and the toilets had no seats.

"Why no seats?" I asked Lisa.

"Could rip off a seat and whack somebody? I don't know."

The nursing station wasn't open, like ours, but encased in chicken-wire glass. Nurses were either in or out. No leaning over the Dutch door to chat on maximum security.

And the rooms were not really rooms. They were cells. They were seclusion rooms, in fact. There wasn't anything in them except bare mattresses with people on them. Unlike our seclusion room, they had windows, but the windows were tiny, high, chicken-wire-enforced, security-screened, barred windows. Most of the doors to the rooms were open, so as we walked down the hall to see Alice, we could see other people lying on their mattresses. Some were naked. Some were not on their mattresses but standing in a corner or curled up against a wall.

That was it. That was all there was. Little bare rooms with one person per room curled up somewhere.

Alice's room didn't smell good. Her walls were smeared with something. So was she. She was sitting on her mattress with her arms wrapped around her knees, and with smears on her arms.

"Hi, Alice," said Georgina.

"That's shit," Lisa whispered to me. "She's been rubbing her shit around."

We stood around outside the doorway. We didn't want to go into the room because of the smell. Alice looked like somebody else, as if she'd gotten a new face. She looked kind of good.

"How's it going?" asked Georgina.

"It's okay," said Alice. Her voice was hoarse. "I'm hoarse," she said. "I've been yelling."

"Right," said Georgina.

Nobody said anything for a minute.

"I'm getting better," said Alice.

"Good," said Georgina.

Lisa tapped her foot on the linoleum. I was feeling faint from trying to breathe without breathing in the smell.

"So," said Georgina. "Well. See you soon, okay?"

"Thanks for coming," said Alice. She unclasped her knees for a few seconds to wave at us.

We went over to the nursing station, where our escort had gone to visit with the staff. We couldn't see our nurse. Georgina rapped on the glass. The person on duty looked up and shook her head at us.

"I just want to get out of here," I said.

Georgina rapped on the glass again. "We want to go back to SB Two," she said loudly.

The person on duty nodded, but our nurse did not appear.

"Maybe they tricked us," said Lisa. "Gonna leave us here."

"That's not funny," I said.

Georgina gave another rat-a-tat to the glass.

"I'll fix it," said Lisa. She pulled her lighter from her pocket and lit up a cigarette.

Immediately two nurses sprang out of the nursing station.

114

"Give me that lighter," said one, while the other grabbed the cigarette.

Lisa smiled. "We need our escort over to SB Two."

The nurses went back into the nursing station.

"No lighters on maximum security. Supervised smoking. I knew that would rouse them." Lisa pulled out another cigarette, then put it back in the pack.

Our nurse came out. "That was a short visit," she said. "How was Alice?"

"She said she was getting better," said Georgina.

"She had shit . . ." I said, but I couldn't describe it.

Our nurse nodded. "It's not that unusual."

The ugly living room, the bedrooms stuffed with bureaus and chairs and blankets and pillows, an aide leaning out of the nursing station talking to Polly, the white chalk in its dish below the blackboard waiting for us to sign ourselves in: home again.

"Oh," I said, sighing several times. I couldn't get enough air in, or get the air in me out.

"What do you think happened to her, anyhow?" said Georgina.

"Something," said Lisa.

"Shit on the wall," I said. "Oh, God. Could that happen to us?"

"She said she was getting better," Georgina said.

"Everything's relative, I guess," said Lisa.

"It couldn't, could it?" I asked.

"Don't let it," said Georgina. "Don't forget it."

The Shadow of the Real

My analyst is dead now. Before he was my analyst, he was my therapist, and I was fond of him. The view from his office on the first floor of the maximum-security-ward building was restful: trees, wind, sky. I was often silent. There was so little silence on our ward. I looked at the trees and said nothing, and he looked at me and said nothing. It was companionable.

Now and then he said something. Once I fell asleep briefly in the chair facing him, after a night full of fighting and yelling on our ward.

"You want to sleep with me," he crowed.

I opened my eyes and looked at him. Sallow, bald early, and with pale pouches under his eyes, he wasn't anybody I wanted to sleep with.

Most of the time, though, he was okay. It calmed me to sit in his office without having to explain myself.

But he couldn't leave well enough alone. He started asking me, "What are you thinking?" I never knew what to say. My head was empty and I liked it that way. Then he began to tell me what I might be thinking. "You seem sad today," he'd say, or "Today, you seem puzzled about something."

Of course I was sad and puzzled. I was eighteen, it was spring, and I was behind bars.

Eventually he said so many wrong things about me that I had to set him right, which was what he'd wanted in the first place. It irritated me that he'd gotten his way. After all, I already knew what I felt; he was the one who didn't know.

His name was Melvin. I felt sorry for him because of this.

Often on the way from our ward to the maximum-security ward, I saw him driving up to his office. Usually he drove a station wagon with fake wood panels, but occasionally he drove a sleek black Buick with oval windows and a vinyl roof. Then one day he shot past me in a pointy green sports car, which he slammed into his parking place with a squeal.

I started to laugh, standing outside his office, because I'd understood something about him, and it was funny. I couldn't wait to tell him.

When I got into his office I said, "You have three cars, right?"

He nodded.

"The station wagon, the sedan, and the sports car."

He nodded again.

"It's the psyche!" I said. I was excited. "See, the station wagon is the ego, sturdy and reliable, and the sedan is the superego, because it's how you want to present yourself, powerful and impressive, and the sports car is the id—it's the id because it's irrepressible and fast and dangerous and maybe a little forbidden." I smiled at him. "It's new, isn't it? The sports car?"

This time he didn't nod.

"Don't you think it's great?" I asked him. "Don't you think it's great that your cars are your psyche?"

He didn't say anything.

It was shortly after this that he began badgering me to go into analysis.

"We aren't getting anywhere," he'd say. "I think analysis is in order."

"Why will it be different?" I wanted to know.

"We aren't getting anywhere," he'd say again.

After a couple of weeks he changed tactics.

"You are the only person in this hospital who could tolerate an analysis," he said.

"Oh yeah? Why's that?" I didn't believe him, but it was intriguing.

"You need a fairly well integrated personality to be in analysis."

I went back to the ward flushed with the idea of my fairly well integrated personality. I didn't tell anyone; that would have been bragging.

If I'd said to Lisa, "I have a fairly well integrated personality and therefore I'm going into analysis with Melvin," she would have made retching sounds and said, "Assholes! They'll say anything!" and I wouldn't have done it.

But I kept it to myself. He'd flattered me—he understood me well enough to know I craved flattery—and in gratitude, I acquiesced.

My view, now, was of a wall, an off-white, featureless wall. No trees, no Melvin patiently looking at me while I looked away. I could feel his presence, though, and it was cold and hard. The only things he said were "Yes?" and

"Could you say more about that?" If I said, "I hate looking at this fucking wall," he'd say, "Could you say more about that?" If I said, "I hate this analysis stuff," he'd say, "Yes?"

Once I asked him, "Why are you so different? You used to be my friend."

"Could you say more about that?"

I started analysis in November, when I was still on group. Five times a week I joined a herd of patients headed for doctors and led by a nurse. But most doctors' offices were in the Administration Building, which was in the opposite direction from the maximum-security ward. So being on group was like being stuck on an inconvenient bus route. I complained. And I got destination privileges.

Now my hour began with a phone call to the nursing station to say I'd arrived in Melvin's office. It ended with my calling to say I was leaving.

Melvin didn't like the phone business. He squinted while I talked on the phone. He kept the phone close to him on his desk. Every day I had to ask him to push it toward me so I could use it.

Perhaps he complained, because soon I got grounds privileges—only to therapy, but it was something. For other activities, I was still on group.

So it was that in December, when I joined Georgina and some other people going to the cafeteria for dinner, I discovered the tunnels.

We say that Columbus discovered America and Newton discovered gravity, as though America and gravity weren't there until Columbus and Newton got wind of them. This was the way I felt about the tunnels. They weren't news to anybody else, but they made such an impression on me that I felt I'd conjured them into being.

It was a typical December day in the Boston area: tin-colored clouds spitting bits of rain mixed with flat watery snowflakes and just enough wind to make you wince.

"Tunnels," said the nurse.

Out the double-locked double doors and down the stairs as usual—our ward was on the second floor for added security. There were many doors in the hallway, one of which went outside. The nurse opened another one, and we went down a second flight of stairs. Then we were in the tunnels.

First their wonderful smell: They smelled of laundry, clean and hot and slightly electrified, like warmed wiring. Then their temperature: eighty at a minimum, and this when it was thirty-three outside, probably twenty-five with wind-chill (though in the innocent sixties, windchill, like digital time, hadn't yet been discovered). Their quavery yellow light, their long yellow-tiled walls and barrel-vaulted ceilings, their forks and twists and roads not taken, whose yellow openings beckoned like shiny open mouths. Here and there, on white tiles embedded in the yellow, were signposts: CAFETERIA, ADMINISTRATION, EAST HOUSE.

"This is great," I said.

"Haven't you been down here before?" asked Georgina.

I asked the nurse, "Do these run under the whole hospital?"

"Yes," she said. "You can get anywhere. It's easy to get lost, though."

"How about the signs?"

"There aren't really enough of them." She giggled; she

was an okay nurse named Ruth. "This one says EAST HOUSE"—
she pointed up—"but then you come to a fork and there isn't
another sign."

"What do you do?"

"You just have to know the way," she said.

"Can I come down here alone?" I asked. I wasn't surprised
when Ruth said I couldn't.

The tunnels became my obsession.

"Anybody free to take me into the tunnels?" I'd ask every
day. About once a week, somebody would take me.

And then there they were, always hot and clean and
yellow and full of promise, always throbbing with heating
and water pipes that sang and whistled as they did their
work. And everything interconnected, everything going on
its own private pathway to wherever it went.

"It's like being in a map—not reading a map but being
inside a map," I said to Ruth one day when she'd taken me
down there. "Like the plan of something rather than the
thing itself." She didn't say anything and I knew I ought to
stop talking about it, but I couldn't. "It's like the essence of
the hospital down here—you know what I mean?"

"Time's up," said Ruth. "I'm on checks in ten minutes."

In February I asked Melvin, "You know those tunnels?"

"Could you tell me more about the tunnels?"

He didn't know about them. If he'd known about them,
he would have said, "Yes?"

"There are tunnels under this entire hospital. Everything
is connected by tunnels. You could get in them and go
anywhere. It's warm and cozy and quiet."

"A womb," said Melvin.

"It's not a womb," I said.

"Yes."

When Melvin said *Yes* without a questioning intonation, he meant *No*.

"It's the opposite of a womb," I said. "A womb doesn't go anywhere." I thought hard about how to explain the tunnels to Melvin. "The hospital is the womb, see. You can't go anywhere, and it's noisy, and you're stuck. The tunnels are like a hospital without the bother."

He said nothing and I said nothing. Then I had another idea.

"Remember the shadows on the wall of the cave?"

"Yes."

He didn't remember them. "Plato said everything in the world is just the shadow of some real thing we can't see. And the real thing isn't like the shadow, it's a kind of essence-thing, like a—" I couldn't think what, for a minute. "Like a super-table."

"Could you say more about that?"

The super-table hadn't been a good example. "It's like a neurosis," I said. I was making this up. "Like when you're angry, and that's the real thing, and what shows is you're afraid of dogs biting you. Because really what you want is to bite everybody. You know?"

Now that I'd said this, I thought it was pretty convincing.

"Why are you angry?" Melvin asked.

He died young, of a stroke. I was his first analytic patient; I found that out after I quit analysis. A year after I got out of the hospital, I quit. I'd had it, finally, with all that messing about in the shadows.

Stigmatography

The hospital had an address, 115 Mill Street. This was to provide some cover if one of us were well enough to apply for a job while still incarcerated. It gave about as much protection as 1600 Pennsylvania Avenue would have.

"Let's see, nineteen years old, living at 1600 Pennsylvania Avenue— Hey! That's the White House!"

This was the sort of look we got from prospective employers, except not pleased.

In Massachusetts, 115 Mill Street is a famous address. Applying for a job, leasing an apartment, getting a driver's license: all problematic. The driver's-license application even asked, Have you ever been hospitalized for mental illness? Oh, no, I just loved Belmont so much I decided to move to 115 Mill Street.

"You're living at One fifteen Mill Street?" asked a small, basement-colored person who ran a sewing-notions shop in Harvard Square, where I was trying to get a job.

"Uh-hunh."

"And how long have you been living there?"

"Oh, a while." I gestured at the past with one hand.

"And I guess you haven't been working for a while?" He leaned back, enjoying himself.

"No," I said. "I've been thinking things over."

I didn't get the job.

As I left the shop my glance met his, and he gave me a look of such terrible intimacy that I cringed. I know what you are, said his look.

What were we, that they could know us so quickly and so well?

We were probably better than we used to be, before we went into the hospital. At a minimum we were older and more self-aware. Many of us had spent our hospital years yelling and causing trouble and were ready to move on to something else. All of us had learned by default to treasure freedom and would do anything we could to get it and keep it.

The question was, What could we do?

Could we get up every morning and take showers and put on clothes and go to work? Could we think straight? Could we not say crazy things when they occurred to us?

Some of us could; some of us couldn't. In the world's terms, though, all of us were tainted.

There's always a touch of fascination in revulsion: Could that happen to me? The less likely the terrible thing is to happen, the less frightening it is to look at or imagine. A person who doesn't talk to herself or stare off into nothingness is therefore more alarming than a person who does. Someone who acts "normal" raises the uncomfortable question, What's the difference between that person and me? which leads to the question, What's keeping me out of the loony bin? This explains why a general taint is useful.

Some people are more frightened than others.

"You spent nearly two years in a loony bin! Why in the world were you in there? I can't believe it!" Translation: If you're crazy, then I'm crazy, and I'm not, so the whole thing must have been a mistake.

"You spent nearly two years in a loony bin? What was wrong with you?" Translation: I need to know the particulars of craziness so I can assure myself that I'm not crazy.

"You spent nearly two years in a loony bin? Hmmm. When was that, exactly?" Translation: Are you still contagious?

I stopped telling people. There was no advantage in telling people. The longer I didn't say anything about it, the farther away it got, until the me who had been in the hospital was a tiny blur and the me who didn't talk about it was big and strong and busy.

I began to feel revulsion too. Insane people: I had a good nose for them and I didn't want to have anything to do with them. I still don't. I can't come up with reassuring answers to the terrible questions they raise.

Don't ask me those questions! Don't ask me what life means or how we know reality or why we have to suffer so much. Don't talk about how nothing feels real, how everything is coated with gelatin and shining like oil in the sun. I don't want to hear about the tiger in the corner or the Angel of Death or the phone calls from John the Baptist. He might give me a call too. But I'm not going to pick up the phone.

If I who was previously revolting am now this far from my crazy self, how much further are you who were never revolting, and how much deeper your revulsion?

September 4, 1968

New England Telephone Co.
165 Franklin Street
Boston, Massachusetts

                    Re: Miss Susanna N. Kaysen
                    ███Callender Street
                    Cambridge, Massachusetts

Gentlemen:

    This is to inform you that Miss Susanna N. Kaysen has been a
patient under my care for psychiatric condition since April 27, 1967.
She is shortly to leave the hospital and reside at the above address.
I feel it important for Miss Kaysen's physical and mental well-being
for us to have easy access to one another via telephone contact. I,
therefore, urge you to give her whatever assistance you can in obtain-
ing a telephone at the earliest possible date.

    I realize that this is and has been a difficult time for the
company because of the recent strike which I am happy to see has been
settled. Again I express my appreciation for whatever you can do to
help Miss Kaysen.

                            Yours sincerely,

                            ████████████████ M.D.
                            Psychiatrist In Charge, SB-II

███/mc

July 10, 1973

Office of the Registry
40 Spring Street
Watertown, Mass. 02172

Dear Sir:

Mrs. Susanna (Kaysen) Wylie was at McLean Hospital
from April 27, 1967, through October 4, 1968. She
has subsequently been married and has managed a
responsible job. At the time of her outright discharge on January 3, 1969, there was no reason why
she could not operate a motor vehicle.

If you have any further questions, please call me.

Sincerely,

███████████ M.D.

██/jbw

cc Susanna Wylie

New Frontiers in
Dental Health

My one-and-a-half-year sentence was running out and it was time to plan my future. I was nearing twenty.

I'd had two jobs in my life: three months selling gourmet cookware, much of which I dropped and broke; and one week typing in the Harvard billing office, terrifying students by sending them term bills for $10,900 that were meant to read $1,900.

I made these mistakes because I was terrified by the supervisor. The supervisor was an elegant and attractive black man who roamed all day among the aisles of typists, watching us work. He smoked while doing this. When I lit a cigarette, he pounced on me.

"You can't smoke," he said.

"But you're smoking."

"Typists are not permitted to smoke."

I looked around the room. All typists were women; all supervisors were men. All supervisors were smoking; all typists were not.

When break time came, at ten-fifteen, the bathroom was stuffed with smoking typists.

"Can't we smoke in the hall?" I asked. There was an ashtray outside the bathroom.

But we couldn't. We had to smoke in the bathroom.

The other problem was clothes.

"No miniskirts," said the supervisor.

This put me in a pickle, as I had only miniskirts, and I had as yet no paycheck. "Why?" I asked.

"No miniskirts," he repeated.

Smoking was Monday, miniskirts was Tuesday. Wednesday I wore a black miniskirt with black tights and hoped for the best.

"No miniskirts," he said.

I scooted to the bathroom for a quick cigarette.

"No smoking except on break," he muttered as he passed my desk on his next round.

This was when I began making my high-priced mistakes.

Thursday he beckoned me over to his desk, where he sat, smoking.

"Making some mistakes," he said. "We can't have that."

"If I could smoke," I said, "I wouldn't make so many."

He just shook his head.

Friday I didn't go in. I didn't call either. I lay in bed smoking and thinking about the office. The more I thought about it the more absurd it became. I couldn't take all those rules seriously. I started to laugh, thinking of the typists jammed into the bathroom, smoking.

But it was my job. Not only that—I was the one person who had trouble with the rules. Everybody else accepted them.

Was this a mark of my madness?

All weekend I thought about it. Was I crazy or right? In 1967, this was a hard question to answer. Even twenty-five years later, it's a hard question to answer.

Sexism! It was pure sexism—isn't that the answer?

It's true, it was sexism. But I'm still having trouble with rules about smoking. Now we've got smokism. It's one of the reasons I became a writer: to be able to smoke in peace.

"A writer," I said, when my social worker asked me what I planned to do when I got out of the hospital. "I'm going to be a writer."

"That's a nice hobby, but how are you going to earn a living?"

My social worker and I did not like each other. I didn't like her because she didn't understand that this was *me*, and I was going to be a writer; I was not going to type term bills or sell au gratin bowls or do any other stupid things. She didn't like me because I was arrogant and uncooperative and probably still crazy for insisting on being a writer.

"A dental technician," she said. "That's the ticket. The training is only one year. I'm sure you'd be able to manage the responsibilities."

"You don't understand," I said.

"No, *you* don't understand," she said.

"I hate the dentist."

"It's nice clean work. You have to be realistic."

"Valerie," I said, when I got back to the ward, "she wants me to be a dental technician. It's impossible."

"Oh?" Valerie didn't seem to understand either. "It's not bad. Nice clean work."

Luckily, I got a marriage proposal and they let me out. In 1968, everybody could understand a marriage proposal.

Topography of the Future

Christmas in Cambridge. The Harvard students from New York and Oregon had switched places with the Columbia and Reed students from Cambridge: vacation musical chairs.

The brother of my friend who was going to die a violent death—but we didn't know that yet; his death was nearly two years in the future—took me to the movies, where I met my husband-to-be. Our marriage as well was two years in the future.

We met in front of the Brattle Theatre. *Les Enfants du Paradis* was playing. And in the bright, dry December air, Cambridge seemed a sort of paradise that evening, busy with lights and Christmas shoppers and a fine dry snow. The snow fell on my future husband's fine blond hair. They'd gone to high school together, my doomed friend's brother and he. Now he was home from Reed for Christmas vacation.

I sat between them in the balcony, where we could smoke. Long before Baptiste lost Garance in the crowd, my future husband had taken my hand in his. He was still holding it when we came out of the theater, and my friend's brother tactfully left us there, in the twirling snowy Cambridge night.

He wouldn't let me go. We were infected by the movie, and Cambridge was beautiful that night, full of possibilities and life. We spent the night together, in an apartment he borrowed from a friend.

He went back to Reed; I went back to selling garlic presses and madeleine pans. Then the future started closing in on me and I forgot about him.

He didn't forget about me. When he graduated that spring and returned to Cambridge, he tracked me down in the hospital. He was going to Paris for the summer, he said, but he would write to me. He wouldn't forget to write, he said.

I paid no attention. He lived in a world with a future and I did not.

When he came back from Paris, things were bad: Torrey's leaving, the question of my bones, the worry over how much time I'd lost in the dentist's chair. I didn't want to see him. I told the staff I was too upset.

"It's impossible! I'm too upset."

We talked on the phone instead. He was moving to Ann Arbor. That was fine with me.

He didn't like Ann Arbor. Eight months later, he was back, wanting to visit again.

Things were not as bad. I had a lot of privileges. We went to movies, we cooked dinner together in his apartment, we watched the body count for the day on the seven o'clock news. At eleven-thirty I'd call a taxi and go back to the hospital.

Late that summer my friend's body was found at the bottom of an elevator shaft. It was a hot summer, and his body was partly decomposed. That was where his future ended, in a basement on a hot day.

One September night I got back to the hospital early, before eleven. Lisa was sitting with Georgina in our room.

"I got a marriage proposal tonight," I said.

"What did you say?" Georgina asked.

"I got a marriage proposal," I said. The second time I said it, I was more surprised by it.

"To him," said Georgina. "What did you say to him?"

"I said Yes," I said.

"You wanna marry him?" Lisa asked.

"Sure," I said. I wasn't completely sure, though.

"And then what?" said Georgina.

"What do you mean?"

"What's going to happen then, after you're married?"

"I don't know," I said. "I haven't thought about it."

"You better think about it," said Lisa.

I tried. I closed my eyes and thought of us in the kitchen, chopping and stirring. I thought of my friend's funeral. I thought of going to movies.

"Nothing," I said. "It's quiet. It's like—I don't know. It's like falling off a cliff." I laughed. "I guess my life will just stop when I get married."

It didn't. It wasn't quiet either. And in the end, I lost him. I did it on purpose, the way Garance lost Baptiste in the crowd. I needed to be alone, I felt. I wanted to be going on alone to my future.

Mind vs. Brain

Whatever we call it—mind, character, soul—we like to think we possess something that is greater than the sum of our neurons and that "animates" us.

A lot of mind, though, is turning out to be brain. A memory is a particular pattern of cellular changes on particular spots in our heads. A mood is a compound of neurotransmitters: Too much acetylcholine, not enough serotonin, and you've got a depression.

So, what's left of mind?

It's a long way from not having enough serotonin to thinking the world is "stale, flat and unprofitable"; even further to writing a play about a man driven by that thought. That leaves a lot of mind room. Something is interpreting the clatter of neurological activity.

But is this interpreter necessarily metaphysical and unembodied? Isn't it probably a number—an enormous number—of brain functions working in parallel? If the entire network of simultaneous tiny actions that constitute a thought were identified and mapped, then "mind" might be visible.

The interpreter is convinced it's unmappable and invisible. "I'm your mind," it claims. "You can't parse *me* into dendrites and synapses."

It's full of claims and reasons. "You're a little depressed because of all the stress at work," it says. (It never says, "You're a little depressed because your serotonin level has dropped.")

Sometimes its interpretations are not credible, as when you cut your finger and it starts yelling, "You're gonna die!" Sometimes its claims are unlikely, as when it says, "Twenty-five chocolate chip cookies would be the perfect dinner."

Often, then, it doesn't know what it's talking about. And when you decide it's wrong, who or what is making that decision? A second, superior interpreter?

Why stop at two? That's the problem with this model. It's endless. Each interpreter needs a boss to report to.

But something about this model describes the essence of our experience of consciousness. There is thought, and then there is thinking about thoughts, and they don't feel the same. They must reflect quite different aspects of brain function.

The point is, the brain talks to itself, and by talking to itself changes its perceptions. To make a new version of the not-entirely-false model, imagine the first interpreter as a foreign correspondent, reporting from the world. The world in this case means everything out- or inside our bodies, including serotonin levels in the brain. The second interpreter is a news analyst, who writes op-ed pieces. They read each other's work. One needs data, the other needs an overview; they influence each other. They get dialogues going.

INTERPRETER ONE: Pain in the left foot, back of heel.
INTERPRETER TWO: I believe that's because the shoe is too tight.

138

INTERPRETER ONE: Checked that. Took off the shoe. Foot still hurts.
INTERPRETER TWO: Did you look at it?
INTERPRETER ONE: Looking. It's red.
INTERPRETER TWO: No blood?
INTERPRETER ONE: Nope.
INTERPRETER TWO: Forget about it.
INTERPRETER ONE: Okay.

A minute later, though, there's another report.

INTERPRETER ONE: Pain in the left foot, back of heel.
INTERPRETER TWO: I know that already.
INTERPRETER ONE: Still hurts. Now it's puffed up.
INTERPRETER TWO: It's just a blister. Forget about it.
INTERPRETER ONE: Okay.

Two minutes later.

INTERPRETER TWO: Don't pick it!
INTERPRETER ONE: It'll feel better if I pop it.
INTERPRETER TWO: That's what you think. Leave it alone.
INTERPRETER ONE: Okay. Still hurts, though.

Mental illness seems to be a communication problem between interpreters one and two.
An exemplary piece of confusion:

INTERPRETER ONE: There's a tiger in the corner.
INTERPRETER TWO: No, that's not a tiger—that's a bureau.
INTERPRETER ONE: It's a tiger, it's a tiger!
INTERPRETER TWO: Don't be ridiculous. Let's go look at it.

Then all the dendrites and neurons and serotonin levels and interpreters collect themselves and trot over to the corner.

If you are not crazy, the second interpreter's assertion, that this is a bureau, will be acceptable to the first interpreter. If you are crazy, the first interpreter's viewpoint, the tiger theory, will prevail.

The trouble here is that the first interpreter actually sees a tiger. The messages sent between neurons are incorrect somehow. The chemicals triggered are the wrong chemicals, or the impulses are going to the wrong connections. Apparently, this happens often, but the second interpreter jumps in to straighten things out.

Think of being in a train, next to another train, in a station. When the other train starts moving, you are convinced that your train is moving. The rattle of the other train feels like the rattle of your train, and you see your train leaving that other train behind. It can take a while—maybe even half a minute—before the second interpreter sorts through the first interpreter's claim of movement and corrects it. That's because it's hard to counteract the validity of sensory impressions. We are designed to believe in them.

The train situation is not the same as an optical illusion. An optical illusion does contain two realities. It's not that the vase is wrong and the faces are right; both are right, and the brain moves between two existing patterns that it recognizes as different. Although you can make yourself dizzy going from vase to faces and back again, you can't undermine your sense of reality in quite such a visceral way as you can with the train.

Sometimes, when you've realized that your train is not really moving, you can spend another half a minute suspended between two realms of consciousness: the one that knows you aren't moving and the one that feels you are. You can flit back and forth between these perceptions and experience a sort of mental vertigo. And if you do this, you are treading on the ground of craziness—a place where false impressions have all the hallmarks of reality.

Freud said psychotics were unanalyzable because they couldn't distinguish between fantasy and reality (tiger vs. bureau), and analysis works on precisely that distinction. The patient must lay out the often fantastic assertions of the first interpreter and scrutinize them with the second. The hope is that the second interpreter has, or will learn to have, the wit and insight to disprove some of the ridiculous claims the first interpreter has made over the years.

You can see why doubting one's own craziness is considered a good sign: It's a sort of flailing response by the second interpreter. What's happening? the second interpreter is saying. He tells me it's a tiger but I'm not convinced; maybe there's something wrong with me. Enough doubt is in there to give "reality" a toehold.

No doubt, no analysis. Somebody who comes in chatting about tigers is going to be offered Thorazine, not the couch.

At that moment, when the doctor suggests Thorazine, what's happening to that doctor's mental map of mental illness? Earlier in the day, the doctor had a map divided into superego, ego, and id, with all kinds of squiggly, perhaps broken, lines running among those three areas. The doctor was treating something he or she calls a psyche or mind. All of a sudden the doctor is preparing to treat a brain. This brain doesn't have a psychelike arrangement, or if it does, that's not where its problem is. This brain has problems that are chemical and electrical.

"It's the reality-testing function," says the doctor. "This brain is bollixed up about reality and I can't analyze it. Those other brains—minds—weren't."

Something's wrong here. You can't call a piece of fruit an apple when you want to eat it and a dandelion when you don't want to eat it. It's the same sort of fruit no matter what your intentions toward it. And how strong is the case for a categorical distinction between brains that know reality and brains that don't? Is a non–reality-recognizing brain truly as different from a reality-recognizing brain as a foot, say, is from a brain? This seems unlikely. Recognizing the agreed-upon version of reality is only one of billions of brain jobs.

If the biochemists were able to demonstrate the physical workings of neuroses (phobias, or difficulties getting pleasure from life), if they could pinpoint the chemicals and impulses and interbrain conversations and information exchanges that constitute these feelings, would the psychoanalysts pack up their ids and egos and retire from the field?

They have partially retired from the field. Depression, manic-depression, schizophrenia: All that stuff they always had trouble treating they now treat chemically. Take two Lithium and don't call me in the morning because there's nothing to say; it's innate.

Some cooperative efforts—the sort the brain makes—would be useful here.

For nearly a century the psychoanalysts have been writing op-ed pieces about the workings of a country they've never traveled to, a place that, like China, has been off-limits. Suddenly, the country has opened its borders and is crawling with foreign correspondents; neurobiologists are filing ten stories a week, filled with new data. These two groups of writers, however, don't seem to read each other's work.

That's because the analysts are writing about a country they call Mind and the neuroscientists are reporting from a country they call Brain.

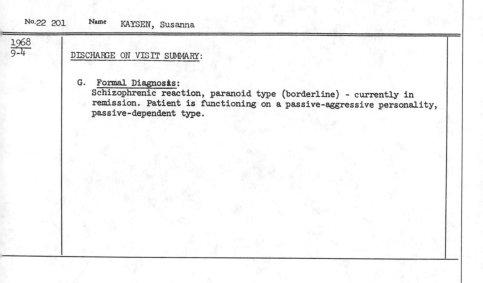

1968
9-4

DISCHARGE ON VISIT SUMMARY:

   G. Formal Diagnosis:
      Schizophrenic reaction, paranoid type (borderline) - currently in
      remission. Patient is functioning on a passive-aggressive personality,
      passive-dependent type.

KAYSEN, Susanna N.   12
Hospital No. 22201

CASE REPORT-CONT'D

       B. Prognosis: The resolution of the depressive affect and
suicidal drive should be expected as a result of the hospitalization. The
degree of personality integration and ego function which may be achieved
for the long term is hard to predict. We may say that with a good
intensive working relationship in therapy and a successful relationship to
the hospital the patient may be able to achieve a more satisfactory means
of adapting. Nevertheless because of the chronicity of the illness and
the basic deficiencies involved in personality structuring, a more complete
recovery is not to be expected at this time. However, the patient may learn
to make more wise choices for herself within the boundaries of her personality
so that she is able to achieve a satisfactory dependent relationship if
necessary which will sustain her for a long period of time.

Borderline Personality Disorder*

An essential feature of this disorder is a pervasive pattern of instability of self-image, interpersonal relationships, and mood, beginning in early adulthood and present in a variety of contexts.

A marked and persistent identity disturbance is almost invariably present. This is often pervasive, and is manifested by uncertainty about several life issues, such as self-image, sexual orientation, long-term goals or career choice, types of friends or lovers to have, and which values to adopt. The person often experiences this instability of self-image as chronic feelings of emptiness and boredom.

Interpersonal relationships are usually unstable and intense, and may be characterized by alternation of the extremes of overidealization and devaluation. These people have difficulty tolerating being alone, and will make frantic efforts to avoid real or imagined abandonment.

Affective instability is common. This may be evidenced by marked mood shifts from baseline mood to depression, irritability, or anxiety, usually lasting a few hours or, only

* From the *Diagnostic and Statistical Manual of Mental Disorders*, 3d edition, revised (1987), pp. 346–47

147

rarely, more than a few days. In addition, these people often have inappropriately intense anger with frequent displays of temper or recurrent physical fights. They tend to be impulsive, particularly in activities that are potentially self-damaging, such as shopping sprees, psychoactive substance abuse, reckless driving, casual sex, shoplifting, and binge eating.

Recurrent suicidal threats, gestures, or behavior and other self-mutilating behavior (e.g., wrist-scratching) are common in the more severe forms of the disorder. This behavior may serve to manipulate others, may be a result of intense anger, or may counteract feelings of "numbness" and depersonalization that arise during periods of extreme stress. . . .

Associated Features. Frequently this disorder is accompanied by many features of other Personality Disorders, such as Schizotypal, Histrionic, Narcissistic, and Antisocial Personality Disorders. In many cases more than one diagnosis is warranted. Quite often social contrariness and a generally pessimistic outlook are observed. Alternation between dependency and self-assertion is common. During periods of extreme stress, transient psychotic symptoms may occur, but they are generally of insufficient severity or duration to warrant an additional diagnosis.

Impairment. Often there is considerable interference with social or occupational functioning.

Complications. Possible complications include Dysthymia [depressive neurosis], Major Depression, Psychoactive Substance Abuse, and psychotic disorders such as Brief Reactive Psychosis. Premature death may result from suicide.

Sex Ratio. The disorder is more commonly diagnosed in women.

Prevalence. Borderline Personality Disorder is apparently common.

Predisposing and Familial Pattern. No information.

Differential Diagnosis. In Identity Disorder there is a similar clinical picture, but Borderline Personality Disorder preempts the diagnosis of Identity Disorder if the criteria for Borderline Personality Disorder are met, the disturbance is sufficiently pervasive and persistent, and it is unlikely that it will be limited to a developmental stage....

My Diagnosis

So these were the charges against me. I didn't read them until twenty-five years later. "A character disorder" is what they'd told me then.

I had to find a lawyer to help me get my records from the hospital; I had to read line 32a of form A1 of the Case Record, and entry G on the Discharge on Visit Summary, and entry B of Part IV of the Case Report; then I had to locate a copy of the *Diagnostic and Statistical Manual of Mental Disorders* and look up Borderline Personality to see what they really thought about me.

It's a fairly accurate picture of me at eighteen, minus a few quirks like reckless driving and eating binges. It's accurate but it isn't profound. Of course, it doesn't aim to be profound. It's not even a case study. It's a set of guidelines, a generalization.

I'm tempted to try refuting it, but then I would be open to the further charges of "defensiveness" and "resistance."

All I can do is give the particulars: an annotated diagnosis.

"[U]ncertainty about several life issues, such as self-image, sexual orientation, long-term goals or career choice, types of friends or lovers to have ..." I relish that last phrase. Its awkwardness (the "to have" seems superfluous) gives it substance and heft. I still have that uncertainty. Is this the type of friend or lover I want to have? I ask myself every time I meet someone new. Charming but shallow; good-hearted but a bit conventional; too handsome for his own good; fascinating but probably unreliable; and so forth. I guess I've had my share of unreliables. More than my share? How many would constitute more than my share?

Fewer than for somebody else—somebody who'd never been called a borderline personality?

That's the nub of my problem here.

If my diagnosis had been bipolar illness, for instance, the reaction to me and to this story would be slightly different. That's a chemical problem, you'd say to yourself, manic-depression, Lithium, all that. I would be blameless, somehow. And what about schizophrenia—that would send a chill up your spine. After all, that's real insanity. People don't "recover" from schizophrenia. You'd have to wonder how much of what I'm telling you is true and how much imagined.

I'm simplifying, I know. But these words taint everything. The fact that I was locked up taints everything.

What does *borderline personality* mean, anyhow?

It appears to be a way station between neurosis and psychosis: a fractured but not disassembled psyche. Though to quote my post-Melvin psychiatrist: "It's what they call people whose lifestyles bother them."

He can say it because he's a doctor. If I said it, nobody would believe me.

An analyst I've known for years said, "Freud and his circle thought most people were hysterics, then in the fifties it was psychoneurotics, and lately, everyone's a borderline personality."

When I went to the corner bookstore to look up my diagnosis in the *Manual*, it occurred to me that I might not find it in there anymore. They do get rid of things—homosexuality, for instance. Until recently, quite a few of my friends would have found themselves documented in that book along with me. Well, they got out of the book and I didn't. Maybe in another twenty-five years I won't be in there either.

"[I]nstability of self-image, interpersonal relationships, and mood . . . uncertainty about . . . long-term goals or career choice . . ." Isn't this a good description of adolescence? Moody, fickle, faddish, insecure: in short, impossible.

"[S]elf-mutilating behavior (e.g., wrist-scratching) . . ." I've skipped forward a bit. This is the one that caught me by surprise as I sat on the floor of the bookstore reading my diagnosis. Wrist-scratching! I thought I'd invented it. Wrist-banging, to be precise.

This is where people stop being able to follow me. This is the sort of stuff you get locked up for. Nobody knew I was doing it, though. I never told anyone, until now.

I had a butterfly chair. In the sixties, everyone in Cambridge had a butterfly chair. The metal edge of its upturned seat was perfectly placed for wrist-banging. I had tried breaking ashtrays and walking on the shards, but I didn't have the nerve to tread firmly. Wrist-banging—slow, steady, mindless—was a better solution. It was cumulative injury, so each bang was tolerable.

A solution to what? I quote from the *Manual*: "This be-

havior may . . . counteract feelings of 'numbness' and depersonalization that arise during periods of extreme stress."

I spent hours in my butterfly chair banging my wrist. I did
it in the evenings, like homework. I'd do some homework,
then I'd spend half an hour wrist-banging, then finish my
homework, then back in the chair for some more banging
before brushing my teeth and going to bed. I banged the
inside, where the veins converge. It swelled and turned a bit
blue, but considering how hard and how much I banged it,
the visible damage was slight. That was yet one more rec-
ommendation of it to me.

I'd had an earlier period of face-scratching. If my fingernails hadn't been quite short, I couldn't have gotten away
with it. As it was, I definitely looked puffy and peculiar the
next day. I used to scratch my cheeks and then rub soap on
them. Maybe the soap prevented me from looking worse.
But I looked bad enough that people asked, "Is something
wrong with your face?" So I switched to wrist-banging.

I was like an anchorite with a hair shirt. Part of the point
was that nobody knew about my suffering. If people knew
and admired—or abominated—me, something important
would be lost.

I was trying to explain my situation to myself. My situation was that I was in pain and nobody knew it; even I had
trouble knowing it. So I told myself, over and over, You are
in pain. It was the only way I could get through to myself
("counteract feelings of 'numbness' "). I was demonstrating,
externally and irrefutably, an inward condition.

"Quite often social contrariness and a generally pessimistic outlook are observed." What do you suppose they mean

by "social contrariness"? Putting my elbows on the table? Refusing to get a job as a dental technician? Disappointing my parents' hope that I would go to a first-rate university?

They don't define "social contrariness," and I can't define it, so I think it ought to be excluded from the list. I'll admit to the generally pessimistic outlook. Freud had one too.

I can honestly say that my misery has been transformed into common unhappiness, so by Freud's definition I have achieved mental health. And my discharge sheet, at line 41, Outcome with Regard to Mental Disorder, reads "Recovered."

Recovered. Had my personality crossed over that border, whatever and wherever it was, to resume life within the confines of the normal? Had I stopped arguing with my personality and learned to straddle the line between sane and insane? Perhaps I'd actually had an identity disorder. "In Identity Disorder there is a similar clinical picture, but Borderline Personality . . . preempts the diagnosis . . . if the disturbance is sufficiently pervasive and . . . it is unlikely that it will be limited to a developmental stage." Maybe I was a victim of improper preemption?

I'm not finished with this diagnosis.

"The person often experiences this instability of self-image as chronic feelings of emptiness or boredom." My chronic feelings of emptiness and boredom came from the fact that I was living a life based on my incapacities, which were numerous. A partial list follows. I could not and did not want to: ski, play tennis, or go to gym class; attend to any subject in school other than English and biology; write papers on any assigned topics (I wrote poems instead of papers for English; I got F's); plan to go or apply to college; give any reasonable explanation for these refusals.

My self-image was not unstable. I saw myself, quite correctly, as unfit for the educational and social systems.

But my parents and teachers did not share my self-image. Their image of me was unstable, since it was out of kilter with reality and based on their needs and wishes. They did not put much value on my capacities, which were admittedly few, but genuine. I read everything, I wrote constantly, and I had boyfriends by the barrelful.

"Why don't you do the assigned reading?" they'd ask. "Why don't you write your papers instead of whatever you're writing—what is that, a short story?" "Why don't you expend as much energy on your schoolwork as you do on your boyfriends?"

By my senior year I didn't even bother with excuses, let alone explanations.

"Where is your term paper?" asked my history teacher.

"I didn't write it. I have nothing to say on that topic."

"You could have picked another topic."

"I have nothing to say on any historical topic."

One of my teachers told me I was a nihilist. He meant it as an insult but I took it as a compliment.

Boyfriends and literature: How can you make a life out of those two things? As it turns out, I did; more literature than boyfriends lately, but I guess you can't have everything ("a generally pessimistic outlook [is] observed").

Back then I didn't know that I—or anyone—could make a life out of boyfriends and literature. As far as I could see, life demanded skills I didn't have. The result was chronic emptiness and boredom. There were more pernicious results as well: self-loathing, alternating with "inappropriately intense anger with frequent displays of temper . . ."

What would have been an appropriate level of intensity for my anger at feeling shut out of life? My classmates were spinning their fantasies for the future: lawyer, ethnobotanist, Buddhist monk (it was a very progressive high school). Even the dumb, uninteresting ones who were there to provide "balance" looked forward to their marriages and their children. I knew I wasn't going to have any of this because I knew I didn't want it. But did that mean I would have nothing?

I was the first person in the history of the school not to go to college. Of course, at least a third of my classmates never finished college. By 1968, people were dropping out daily.

Quite often now, people say to me, when I tell them I didn't go to college, "Oh, how marvelous!" They wouldn't have thought it was so marvelous back then. They didn't; my classmates were just the sorts of people who now tell me how marvelous I am. In 1966, I was a pariah.

What was I going to do? a few of my classmates asked.

"I'm going to join the WACs," I told one guy.

"Oh, yeah? That will be an interesting career."

"Just kidding," I said.

"Oh, uh, you mean you're not, really?"

I was stunned. Who did they think I was?

I'm sure they didn't think about me much. I was that one who wore black and—really, I've heard it from several people—slept with the English teacher. They were all seventeen and miserable, just like me. They didn't have time to wonder why I was a little more miserable than most.

Emptiness and boredom: what an understatement. What I felt was complete desolation. Desolation, despair, and depression.

Isn't there some other way to look at this? After all, angst of these dimensions is a luxury item. You need to be well fed, clothed, and housed to have time for this much self-pity. And the college business: My parents wanted me to go, I didn't want to go, and I didn't go. I got what I wanted. Those who don't go to college have to get jobs. I agreed with all this. I told myself all this over and over. I even got a job—my job breaking au gratin dishes.

But the fact that I couldn't hold my job was worrisome. I was probably crazy. I'd been skirting the idea of craziness for a year or two; now I was closing in on it.

Pull yourself together! I told myself. Stop indulging yourself. There's nothing wrong with you. You're just wayward.

One of the great pleasures of mental health (whatever that is) is how much less time I have to spend thinking about myself.

I have a few more annotations to my diagnosis.

"The disorder is more commonly diagnosed in women."

Note the construction of that sentence. They did not write, "The disorder is more common in women." It would still be suspect, but they didn't even bother trying to cover their tracks.

Many disorders, judging by the hospital population, were more commonly diagnosed in women. Take, for example, "compulsive promiscuity."

How many girls do you think a seventeen-year-old boy would have to screw to earn the label "compulsively promiscuous"? Three? No, not enough. Six? Doubtful. Ten? That sounds more likely. Probably in the fifteen-to-twenty range, would be my guess—if they ever put that label on boys, which I don't recall their doing.

And for seventeen-year-old girls, how many boys?

In the list of six "potentially self-damaging" activities favored by the borderline personality, three are commonly associated with women (shopping sprees, shoplifting, and eating binges) and one with men (reckless driving). One is not "gender-specific," as they say these days (psychoactive substance abuse). And the definition of the other (casual sex) is in the eye of the beholder.

Then there is the question of "premature death" from suicide. Luckily, I avoided it, but I thought about suicide a lot. I'd think about it and make myself sad over my premature death, and then I'd feel better. The idea of suicide worked on me like a purgative or a cathartic. For some people it's different—Daisy, for instance. But was her death really "premature"? Ought she to have sat in her eat-in kitchen with her chicken and her anger for another fifty years? I'm assuming she wasn't going to change, and I may be wrong. She certainly made that assumption, and she may also have been wrong. And if she'd sat there for only thirty years, and killed herself at forty-nine instead of at nineteen, would her death still be "premature"?

I got better and Daisy didn't and I can't explain why. Maybe I was just flirting with madness the way I flirted with my teachers and my classmates. I wasn't convinced I was crazy, though I feared I was. Some people say that having any conscious opinion on the matter is a mark of sanity, but I'm not sure that's true. I still think about it. I'll always have to think about it.

I often ask myself if I'm crazy. I ask other people too.

"Is this a crazy thing to say?" I'll ask before saying something that probably isn't crazy.

I start a lot of sentences with "Maybe I'm totally nuts," or "Maybe I've gone 'round the bend."

If I do something out of the ordinary—take two baths in one day, for example—I say to myself: Are you crazy?

It's a common phrase, I know. But it means something particular to me: the tunnels, the security screens, the plastic forks, the shimmering, ever-shifting borderline that like all boundaries beckons and asks to be crossed. I do not want to cross it again.

Farther on, Down the Road, You Will Accompany Me

Most of us got out eventually. Georgina and I kept in touch.

For a while she lived in a women's commune in north Cambridge. She came over to my apartment one day and terrorized my upstairs neighbor, who was making bread.

"You're doing that wrong!" Georgina said. She and I were having a cup of tea upstairs while my neighbor kneaded the dough.

"Let me show you," said Georgina. She pushed my neighbor out of the way and started flinging the dough around on the counter.

My neighbor was a mild-mannered woman who never did anything graceless or rude. Consequently, most people were polite to her.

"You really have to beat it up," said Georgina, doing so.

"Oh," said my neighbor. She was about ten years older than Georgina and I, and she'd been making bread for all those years.

After she'd given the bread a good beating, Georgina said she had to leave.

"I have never been treated that way," said my neighbor. She seemed more astonished than angry.

Then Georgina got involved in a consciousness-raising

group. She pestered me to come. "You'll love it," she said.

The women made me feel inadequate. They knew how to disassemble car engines and climb mountains. I was the only married one. I could see that Georgina had a certain cachet because of her craziness; somehow, this cachet did not apply to me. But I went often enough to become suspicious of marriage, and of my husband in particular. I picked stupid fights with him. It was hard to find something to fight about. He did the cooking and the shopping, and he did a fair amount of cleaning too. I spent most of my time reading and painting watercolors.

Luckily, Georgina got herself a husband as well and dropped out of the group before I could pick a really destructive fight.

Then we had to go visit their farm in western Massachusetts.

Georgina's husband was pale and slight and unmemorable. But she had also gotten a goat. Georgina, the husband, and the goat lived in a barn on a few acres of scrub land at the foot of a small mountain. The day we visited was cold, though it was May, and they were busy fitting glazing into their windows. They had six-over-six window frames, so this was quite a chore.

We watched while they puttied and fitted. The goat stood in her room near the door and watched as well. Finally, Georgina said it was time for lunch. She made a pressure cooker full of sweet potatoes. That was lunch. There was some maple syrup for topping. The goat had bananas.

After lunch, Georgina said, "Want to see the goat dance?"

The goat's name was Darling. She was the color of ginger and had long hairy ears.

Georgina held a sweet potato up in the air. "Dance, Darling," she said.

The goat stood on her hind legs and chased after the sweet potato, which Georgina kept moving away from her. Her long ears swayed as she hopped, and she pawed the air with her front legs. Her hooves were black and sharp; they looked as though they could do a lot of damage. Indeed, when she lost her footing, which she did a few times, and a hoof grazed the edge of the kitchen counter, it cut a groove in the wood.

"Give it to her," I said. Something about the goat dancing made me want to cry.

They moved west, to Colorado, where the land was better. Georgina called once or twice from a pay phone. They had no telephone of their own. I don't know what happened to the goat.

A few years after Georgina went west, I ran into Lisa in Harvard Square. She had a little toast-colored boy with her, about three years old.

I hugged her. "Lisa," I said, "I'm so happy to see you."

"This is my kid," she said. "Isn't it crazy that I have a kid?" She laughed. "Aaron, say hello." He didn't; he put his face behind her leg.

She looked exactly the same: skinny, yellow, cheerful.

"What have you been doing?" I asked.

"The kid," she said. "That's all you can do."

"What about the father?"

"Later for him. I got rid of him." She put her hand on the boy's head. "We don't need him, do we?"

"Where are you living?" I wanted to know everything about her.

"You won't believe this." Lisa pulled out a Kool and lit up. "I'm living in Brookline. I'm a suburban matron in Brookline. I've got the kid, I take the kid to nursery school, I've got an apartment, I've got furniture. Fridays we go to temple."

"Temple!" This amazed me. "Why?"

"I want—" Lisa faltered. I'd never before seen her at a loss for words. "I want us to be a real family, with furniture, and all that. I want him to have a real life. And temple helps. I don't know why, but it helps."

I stared at Lisa, trying to imagine her in temple with her dark-skinned son. I noticed she was wearing some jewelry— a ring with two sapphires, a gold chain around her neck.

"What's with the jewelry?" I asked.

"Presents from Grandma, right?" She addressed this to the kid. "Everything changes when you have children," she told me.

I didn't know what to say to that. I'd decided not to have any. And it didn't look like my marriage was going to last, either.

We were standing in the middle of Harvard Square in front of the subway entrance. Suddenly, Lisa leaned close to me and said, "Wanna see something fantastic?" Her voice had the old quiver of mischief in it. I nodded.

She pulled up her shirt, a T-shirt advertising a bagel shop in Brookline, and grabbed hold of the flesh of her abdomen.

Then she pulled. Her skin was like an accordion; it kept expanding, more and more, until she was holding the flap of skin a foot away from her body. She let go and it subsided, somewhat wrinkled at first but then settling back on her bones, looking perfectly normal.

"Wow!" I said.

"Kids," said Lisa. "That's what happens." She laughed. "Say good-bye, Aaron."

"Bye," he said, surprising me.

They were going back to Brookline on the subway. At the top of the stairs Lisa turned around toward me again.

"You ever think of those days in there, in that place?" she asked.

"Yes," I answered. "I do think of them."

"Me too." She shook her head. "Oh, well," she said rather jauntily. Then the two of them went down the stairs, underground.

Girl, Interrupted

The Vermeer in the Frick is one of three, but I didn't notice the other two the first time I went there. I was seventeen and in New York with my English teacher, who hadn't yet kissed me. I was thinking of that future kiss, which I knew was coming, as I left the Fragonards behind and walked into the hall leading to the courtyard—that dim corridor where the Vermeers gleam against the wall.

Besides the kiss, I was thinking of whether I could graduate from high school if for the second year in a row I failed biology. I was surprised to be failing it, because I loved it; I'd loved it the first time I failed it too. My favorite part was gene-recession charts. I liked working out the sequence of blue eyes in families that had no characteristics except blue eyes and brown eyes. My family had a lot of characteristics—achievements, ambitions, talents, expectations—that all seemed to be recessive in me.

I walked past the lady in yellow robes and the maid bringing her a letter, past the soldier with a magnificent hat and the girl smiling at him, thinking of warm lips, brown eyes, blue eyes. Her brown eyes stopped me.

It's the painting from whose frame a girl looks out, ignoring her beefy music teacher, whose proprietary hand rests on her chair. The light is muted, winter light, but her face is bright.

I looked into her brown eyes and I recoiled. She was warning me of something—she had looked up from her work to warn me. Her mouth was slightly open, as if she had just drawn a breath in order to say to me, "Don't!"

I moved backward, trying to get beyond the range of her urgency. But her urgency filled the corridor. "Wait," she was saying, "wait! Don't go!"

I didn't listen to her. I went out to dinner with my English teacher, and he kissed me, and I went back to Cambridge and failed biology, though I did graduate, and, eventually, I went crazy.

Sixteen years later I was in New York with my new, rich boyfriend. We took many trips, which he paid for, although spending money made him queasy. On our trips, he often attacked my character—that character once diagnosed as disordered. Sometimes I was too emotional, other times too cold and judgmental. Whichever he said, I'd comfort him by telling him it was okay to spend money. Then he would stop attacking me, which meant we could stay together and begin the spending-and-attack cycle on some future trip.

It was a beautiful October day in New York. He had attacked and I had comforted and now we were ready to go out.

"Let's go to the Frick," he said.

"I've never been there," I said. Then I thought maybe I had been. I didn't say anything; I'd learned not to discuss my doubts.

When we got there I recognized it. "Oh," I said. "There's a painting I love here."

"Only one?" he said. "Look at these Fragonards."

I didn't like them. I left the Fragonards behind and walked into the hall leading to the courtyard.

She had changed a lot in sixteen years. She was no longer urgent. In fact, she was sad. She was young and distracted, and her teacher was bearing down on her, trying to get her to pay attention. But she was looking out, looking for someone who would see her.

This time I read the title of the painting: *Girl Interrupted at Her Music*.

Interrupted at her music: as my life had been, interrupted in the music of being seventeen, as her life had been, snatched and fixed on canvas: one moment made to stand still and to stand for all the other moments, whatever they would be or might have been. What life can recover from that?

I had something to tell her now. "I see you," I said.

My boyfriend found me crying in the hallway.

"What's the matter with you?" he asked.

"Don't you see, she's trying to get out," I said, pointing at her.

He looked at the painting, he looked at me, and he said, "All you ever think about is yourself. You don't understand anything about art." He went off to look at a Rembrandt.

I've gone back to the Frick since then to look at her and at the two other Vermeers. Vermeers, after all, are hard to come by, and the one in Boston has been stolen.

The other two are self-contained paintings. The people in

them are looking at each other—the lady and her maid, the soldier and his sweetheart. Seeing them is peeking at them through a hole in a wall. And the wall is made of light—that entirely credible yet unreal Vermeer light.

Light like this does not exist, but we wish it did. We wish the sun could make us young and beautiful, we wish our clothes could glisten and ripple against our skins, most of all, we wish that everyone we knew could be brightened simply by our looking at them, as are the maid with the letter and the soldier with the hat.

The girl at her music sits in another sort of light, the fitful, overcast light of life, by which we see ourselves and others only imperfectly, and seldom.

KAYSEN, Susanna # 22 201

ADDITIONAL DIAGNOSES, OTHER CONDITIONS, THIS INSTITUTION

A. DIAGNOSIS	B. DATE	A. DIAGNOSIS	B. DATE

OPERATION PERFORMED AT THIS INSTITUTION DURING THIS ADMISSION

A. OPERATION	B. DATE	A. OPERATION	B. DATE

SPECIAL DIAGNOSTIC AND THERAPEUTIC PROCEDURES, THIS ADMISSION

A. PROCEDURE	B. DATE	A. OPERATION	B. DATE
IPS 5x/wk GPS 1x/wk Drug:Chlorpromazine			

RESERVED

DIAGNOSIS AT DISCHARGE, MENTAL DISORDER	41. OUTCOME WITH REGARD TO MENTAL DISORDER
Borderline Personality	**Recovered**

DURING THIS ADMISSION, NUMBER OF

A. VISITS	B. PERIODS OF FAMILY CARE	C. PAROLES	D. ABSENCES WITHOUT AUTHORITY	E. ESCAPES
1	0	0	0	0

DURING THIS ADMISSION, NUMBER OF DAYS SPENT

A. ON BOOKS	B. IN RESIDENCE	C. ON AUTHORIZED LEAVE	D. ON ELOPEMENT
617	496	121	0

LEGAL STATUS AT DISCHARGE	45. SURVIVAL AT DISCHARGE	46A. LAST BOOK CLASSIFICATION	B. DATE BEGAN
Voluntary	**Living**	**On Visit**	**September 4, 1968**

DESTINATION	48. DATE DISCHARGED
Apartment	**January 3, 1969**

FOR DEATHS, COPY FROM DEATH CERTIFICATE

A. DIRECT CAUSE OF DEATH	B. ASSOCIATED SIGNIFICANT CONDITIONS
DUE IN TURN TO ANTECEDENT CAUSES (1) (2)	

0. MEDICAL EXAMINER'S CASE	51. AUTOPSY	52. PLACE OF BURIAL
YES ☐ NO ☐	YES ☐ NO ☐	

Acknowledgments

My thanks to Jill Ker Conway, Maxine Kumin, and Susan Ware for their early encouragement; to Gerald Berlin for his legal help; and to Julie Grau for her enthusiasm and her good care of both book and author.

I am most grateful to Robin Becker, Robin Desser, Michael Downing, Lyda Kuth, and Jonathan Matson for their insights, humor, and true-blue friendship.

Acknowledgments

About the Author

Susanna Kaysen lives in
Cambridge, Massachusetts.